ANIRUDH ARORA
AND HARDEEP SINGH KOHLI

FOOD *of the*
GRAND TRUNK
ROAD

Recipes of rural India, from
Bengal to the Punjab

NEW
HOLLAND

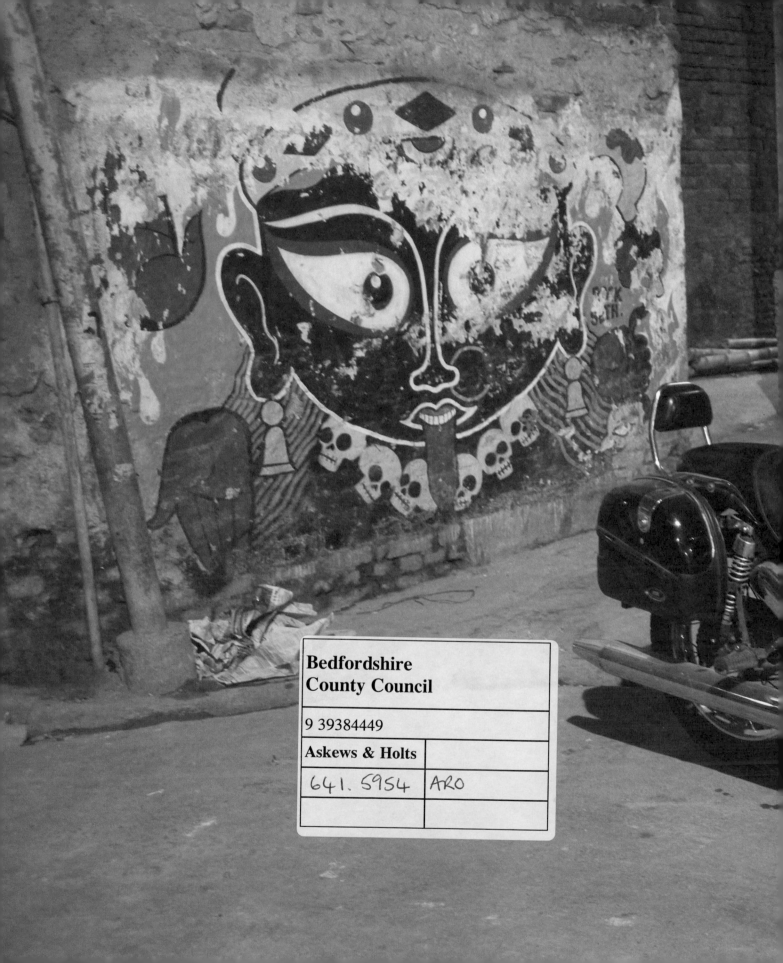

First published in the UK in 2011 by
New Holland Publishers (UK) Ltd
London   Cape Town   Sydney   Auckland

Garfield House, 86–88 Edgware Road
London W2 2EA
United Kingdom
www.newhollandpublishers.com

80 McKenzie Street
Cape Town 8001
South Africa

Unit 1, 66 Gibbes Street
Chatswood, NSW 2067
Australia

218 Lake Road
Northcote, Auckland
New Zealand

ISBN 978 1 84773 968 1

Publisher: Clare Sayer
Production: Laurence Poos
Food Photography: Karen Thomas
Location Photography: Oliver Sinclair
Design: Jacqui Caulton
Prop Stylist: Liz Belton
Food Stylist: Sunil Vijayakar

1 3 5 7 9 10 8 6 4 2

Reproduction by PDQ Digital Media Solution Ltd, UK
Printed and bound by Tien Wah Press, Singapore

The map used on pages 27, 65, 109, 137, 147 and 163 is taken from a historical map of India from 1882
(source: Wikimedia Commons). It is used for decorative purposes only and is not intended to be an
accurate representation of any current geographical or political boundaries.

CONTENTS

FOREWORD

ABOUT 20 YEARS AGO I dreamt of creating a concept that reflected the vast cultural and culinary heritage that is embodied along India's arterial route. Two decades later, Moti Mahal's wonderfully talented head chef Anirudh Arora and writer and broadcaster Hardeep Singh Kohli, whose fathers were in the same Indian regiment, have written this book. *Food of the Grand Trunk Road* is a unique culinary reflection of India's oldest and longest major road. Built in the 16th century by Emperor Sher Shah Suri to connect Agra with his hometown, Sasaram, the Grand Trunk Road now covers 2,500 km from Calcutta to Afghanistan. Having travelled the length of the route, once described by Rudyard Kipling as 'The River of Life', Anirudh has showcased the recipes inspired by those passed down among generations of families, villagers and vendors, whilst Hardeep's words have brought them brilliantly to life. Anirudh has chosen recipes that define the journey from West Bengal, through Benares on the banks of the Ganges, on to Delhi, home of emperors and frontier cuisine, up to Amritsar where the dhaba wallas still deliver multi-layered parathas, through the hunting country of the Punjab, the rugged mountains of Peshawar's Khyber Pass and into the heart of Kabul. Grand Trunk Road food satisfies the tastebuds with the sweets of Bengal, the tangy and spicy dishes of Uttar Pradesh, Mughlai cuisine and Murgh Makhani from the original Moti Mahal in Delhi. It showcases the richness of flavours created for royalty, Indian rural cooking, the biryanis of Lucknow and Punjabi tikkis. There are the robust dishes of the tandoors and the delicate lightness of seasonal vegetables. In every city and village along the GT Road, cooking special dishes for festivals and family occasions is an integral part of life. This is a culinary narrative highlighting long-forgotten recipes; a celebration of the rural bounty of India and its richly woven history and I hope it will create as many memories for you as these dishes have for me.

Puri, Moti Mahal

INTRODUCTION

Hardeep Singh Kohli and Anirudh Arora have joined forces to write this book, bringing together their vastly different experiences and backgrounds — Hardeep was brought up in Glasgow but has always been aware of his Indian heritage while Ani, born in India, has brought his heritage to Britain. What they share, however, is an intense love of the forgotten dishes of the real India. Here, Hardeep asks Anirudh what the Grand Trunk Road means to him.

Hardeep: How did an Indian chef like you end up cooking in the heart of London?

Anirudh: I spent five years at the Oberoi in Calcutta and decided that was enough time there. I had a choice: stay in India and become an executive chef, which would have meant cooking food from all over the world, or move to London, where I knew I could really focus on Indian food. The appetite for Indian food is bigger in London than anywhere else, possibly even bigger than in India.

Hardeep: Really?

Anirudh: Well in India you don't have to choose Indian food — it's all there is, it's necessary to eat it. Whereas in the UK there is a genuine desire to eat Indian food. There is such a wide range of cuisines on offer which means that the quality of Indian food offered in London is better comparatively than the food in India.

Hardeep: Tell me your story...

Anirudh: I was born in Delhi. My father was in the army and my mother was a professor of zoology. When I was a boy it was decided that I would either be an engineer or a doctor, even before I was born! Just like in the Hindi movies. My mum wanted me to be a doctor and my dad wanted me to be an engineer. So obviously, as a kid, you decide that you don't want to be what your parents want you to be. My dad then tried to make me become an army officer so he sent me to Bangalore to sit the entrance exam for the army. But instead of sitting that exam I applied to a hotel management college.

Hardeep: Whenever I have eaten food that you have created, I always have the feeling that the love of food is inside you rather than something you've learnt.

Anirudh: To cook good food you need to eat good food. As my father was in the Indian Army we were well looked after. There was the officer's mess... amazing silver plates and cutlery... it was really special. And that was the first time I ever saw ice cream, hand churned for three hours by some private.

18

Hardeep: Can you remember the first meal that had a real impact on you?

Anirudh: It wasn't a meal actually, it was breakfast. In the mess it was always English breakfast. Scrambled eggs, griddled tomatoes and mushrooms. And I had Marmite… you have to understand that back in those days there was no Marmite in India. Marmite was a big thing. There is no factory, it's still imported. My father told me only the top people eat Marmite. I don't know why he told me that! Perhaps because it was packed with Vitamin B! That breakfast changed me a lot – I was about nine years old.

Hardeep: When did you realise that you were going to become a chef?

Anirudh: I wasn't great at school, so every now and again I would duck out of class and go and watch a movie. On the way back to school I'd pass a tiny petrol station – more a single petrol pump really.

There was this guy outside with a little barrow. All he sold was omelette and bread. Masala omelette and bread... I used to love eating that – I started to enjoy it more than the movie I had escaped school to see. I think that is where my love affair with food started. One day we didn't have enough money for the movie tickets so this friend of mine and I decided to go home and cook something. Although we didn't have enough money for the movie we had just about enough to buy two legs of chicken. We decided to make chicken curry.

Hardeep: How old were you?
Anirudh: Maybe 14. I had NO idea how to cook a chicken curry. My friend (and he's still a good friend) told me that he had cooked a chicken curry – just once.

Hardeep: He's probably a doctor or an engineer now, like a good Indian son!

Anirudh: No, he's a businessman, making plenty of money. Anyway, we got our heads together and made chicken curry.

Hardeep: How was it?

Anirudh: It was good, actually. We fried the onions and then added some garlic. I wanted to add tomatoes but he wanted me to wait till the onions and garlic had cooked. We had a fight about it and I said that since it was my house we would cook it my way. Unfortunately when we came to taste the curry there were whole chunks of garlic in it. But otherwise it tasted pretty good. As we tasted it he said 'I told you so'. And he was right. I should have fried that garlic a bit longer. I've never forgotten that experience.

Hardeep: Tell me about your relationship with the Grand Trunk Road. Why did you send me all the way along it through a particularly cold North Indian winter?

Anirudh: I love food. I'm a north Indian, a Punjabi. Punjabi food is limited — I love it but it is limited. The GT Road defines our menu, both at Moti Mahal and for Punjabis generally; it gives the food character, a story. The GT Road has inspired so many lives, so many stories for so many years. And it has inspired me.

Hardeep: Tell me about the road itself.

Anirudh: The GT Road goes through Delhi where I was born. I studied in Lucknow — the GT passes through there. I spent time in Calcutta where the road starts or ends, depending on your journey. I remember once I drove on a scooter from Lucknow to Delhi — 571 km in a single day. It was an unforgettable journey. I set off at five in the morning and at 7.30pm we reached Delhi. We had food at every stop — the most amazing street food and snacks — too many to remember. We had watermelon... you know in India these guys sit by the roadside with mountains of watermelons. When you stop they just slice one open for you and you eat it. There's no better way to clear the taste of dust from your mouth! It was the best watermelon I have ever tasted.

Hardeep: Didn't you fall in love in Calcutta?

Anirudh: Yes, I met my wife there. I was a chef at The Oberoi Grand, the best hotel in Calcutta. We were both working at the hotel. I was a trainee chef and she was the training manager.

Hardeep: So you fell in love with your boss?

Anirudh: I've never thought about it like that! We started going out to the movies and then stopping for egg rolls, kathi rolls. They don't call them kathi rolls in Calcutta. Just rolls. We ate a lot of rolls.

There was good food everywhere, Chinatown in Calcutta is amazing. It's less Chinese and more Indo-Chinese food. So I have some very fond memories of Chinatown.

Hardeep: There's a lot of history on the Grand Trunk Road.

Anirudh: It's always been in the back of my mind. When you study at primary school in India you hear a lot about the Grand Trunk Road. Almost everyone calls it GT Road. If you want to travel anywhere in North India you travel on the GT Road. It's the lifeline of north India. So if there are millions and millions of people travelling up and down that road then it has to mean something – it creates its own story. And in India, everyone loves food. On the GT Road, food is happening almost everywhere. There are these dhabas on the GT Road. These are some of the most inspirational places I have eaten at. People in the UK talk about organic food. I never heard the term organic food before I came to the UK. Why? Because everything in and around the GT Road is organic. The dhaba is at the end of a keth, a farm. If the dhaba owner needs any mooli, green chillies, tomatoes, anything, he just opens his back door and it's all there, growing in the ground. There are poultry, eggs, milk and butter all nearby. On the GT Road when they talk about fresh butter they mean butter that was churned half an hour ago. Delicious – straight into your dal makhani.

Hardeep: You have a lot of dishes on the menu from Kashmir and Kabul. I never realised the GT stretched so far east. You can't have tasted those sorts of dishes growing up?

Anirudh: Maybe not growing up but my father was posted near the border in Kashmir. There was some exchange of food over the border, communities exist either side. This is one of the fantastic things about Indian food – it has changed and developed over centuries with every invasion, every migration. After the troubles in Afghanistan a lot of the Kabul Sikhs migrated to Delhi, near where I grew up. Though they are Sikhs they have lived in Afghanistan for generations. They brought their food culture with them. They cook Kabuli food and that food can now be found in West Delhi, where these migrants settled. I remember coming home one evening and seeing this man with his stall. I didn't recognise what he was cooking. I looked closer and saw that it was lamb's liver wrapped in fat – nothing else. Served with chutney and naan – but not naan the way I knew it – Kabuli naan is leavened. It's thick and soft, like a pillow.

Hardeep: How does the food change as you travel across the GT Road?

Anirudh: Food changes with the geography. As the landscape changes so does the food. Calcutta is close to the sea so fish is abundant. They have more rivers in Bengal and so rice is their staple rather than wheat. As you travel into central north India there are fewer rivers and less flowing water is available. So they grow more wheat. Mustard leaves are a major crop so mustard oil is used a lot in the cooking. In Uttar Pradesh there is a big Nawabi influence – the Nawabs swept eastwards. Here the kebabs aren't cooked in a clay oven, they are cooked on a steel pan, a tava. Delhi is a metropolitan city, influenced by a range of food cultures. Moving onwards you reach the Punjab, the most fertile state in India, where you will find an abundance of vegetables. The climate suits dairy farming so there is plenty of milk and butter in the cooking.

Hardeep: Whereas Kashmir has a much harsher climate so they use a lot of dried vegetables in their cooking. Isn't the famous Kashmiri chilli dried?

Anirudh: Indeed. They also use a lot of meat since it's more difficult to grow vegetables. Similarly in Afghanistan, there are very few vegetables. They have lots of wheat and so plenty of breads and meat, mostly goat. So you can see the food changing with the geography, with the road. For me, though, the Punjab will always be the most important area, from a culinary point of view, which is why I have featured so many recipes from that region, both from India and Pakistan, in this book.

Hardeep: We've ended the book with a triumphant chapter on the food of the Punjab; though not technically the end of the GT Road, it is a fitting end to a magnificent journey across northern India.

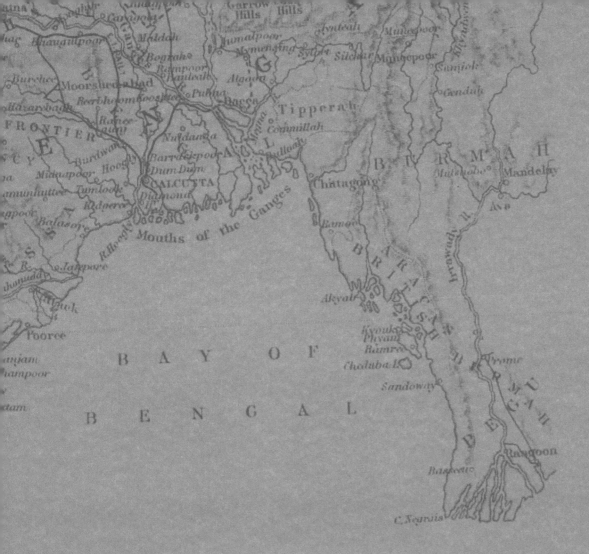

BENGAL & BIHAR

Bengal is predominantly a rice and mustard growing region, with a number of rivers including the Ganges and the Brahmputra crisscrossing the countryside. The main food staples are rice, seafood, green Bengal gram and sweets based on curdled milk. A meal without sweets is incomplete. Bengali dishes are generally flavoured with mustard. Bihar is on the Gangetic plains of central & eastern India, where farming carries the economy. Here you will find wheat, rice, pulses, river fish and vegetables.

Aloo Dimer Jhol

Egg curry with potatoes

SERVES 4

2 small potatoes, peeled

oil, for shallow frying

8 hard-boiled eggs, peeled

4 garlic cloves

I onion, chopped

3 tomatoes, roughly chopped

I bay leaf

I cinnamon stick

3 green cardamom pods

3 cloves

2.5-cm/I-inch piece ginger,
peeled and chopped

2 green chillies, slit lengthways

½ teaspoon ground turmeric

I teaspoon ground cumin

I teaspoon chilli powder

salt, to taste

I tablespoon chopped
fresh coriander

Slice the potatoes lengthways. Heat some oil in a non-stick frying pan and shallow-fry the potatoes over a low heat until just cooked through. Drain on kitchen paper and set aside. Fry the eggs, whole, in the same oil as you cooked the potatoes for 2–3 minutes and set aside.

Put the garlic cloves, chopped onion and tomatoes in a blender or food processor and blend until you have a smooth purée. Set aside.

Add a little more oil to the pan and, once hot, add the bay leaf, cinnamon stick, green cardamom pods and cloves, and cook for a couple of minutes until the flavours infuse. Add the ginger and green chillies and cook for 2 minutes. Add the tomato and onion purée, cover and cook on a medium heat for 10–12 minutes, stirring occasionally.

Add the turmeric, cumin, chilli powder and salt. Add 250 ml water and gently simmer for a further 8–10 minutes, until the mixture thickens. Add the potatoes and eggs and cook for a further 5 minutes. Serve sprinkled with chopped fresh coriander.

Mangsho Ghugni

Lamb and chickpea curry

SERVES 4

400 g/14 oz chickpeas (dried not tinned)

50 ml/2 fl oz mustard oil

2 bay leaves

3 green cardamom pods

3 cloves

1 cinnamon stick

1 teaspoon cumin seeds

1 onion, chopped

1 kg/2¼ lb boneless lamb from the leg, cut into 2.5-cm/1-inch pieces

1 tablespoon ginger and garlic paste (see Note)

½ teaspoon ground turmeric

1 teaspoon ground coriander

1 teaspoon chilli powder

½ teaspoon ground cumin

2 tomatoes, finely chopped

salt, to taste

1 teaspoon garam masala

few sprigs fresh coriander, chopped

Soak the chickpeas in water overnight. Boil in fresh water for about 1–1½ hours until soft. Drain, reserving the cooking liquid, and set aside.

Heat the oil in a large pan and add the bay leaves, green cardamom pods, cloves and cinnamon stick. Allow to infuse. Add the cumin seeds and once they have crackled, add the chopped onion and cook until golden brown. Add the lamb and cook over a high heat until browned.

Add the ginger and garlic paste and cook for 2–3 minutes. Add the ground turmeric, ground coriander, chilli powder, ground cumin and salt. Mix well. Add chopped tomatoes and cook until soft. Add enough of the chickpea cooking water to cover the lamb and cook for 25–30 minutes over a medium heat.

Add the cooked chickpeas and cook for 10–12 minutes, until the meat is tender. Add a little more water if it looks too dry. Adjust the seasoning and sprinkle over the garam masala and chopped fresh coriander.

Note Ginger and garlic paste is a simple paste made from roughly two-thirds garlic and one-third peeled ginger, peeled and blended with enough oil and water to make a smooth paste. It should keep in an airtight container in the fridge for up to week. It is also available ready-made in jars from good supermarkets or Indian grocers.

Kofee Aloo Jhol

Fish and cauliflower curry

SERVES 4

2 teaspoons chilli powder

I teaspoon ground turmeric

salt, to taste

4 fish steaks (eg sea bass)

2 medium potatoes

I cauliflower, broken into florets

5-cm/2-inch piece ginger, peeled and chopped

I teaspoon cumin seeds

100 ml/3½ fl oz mustard oil

2 bay leaves

3 green cardamom pods

I cinnamon stick

3 cloves

I teaspoon onion seeds

I teaspoon ground coriander

I lemon

Mix together ¼ teaspoon chilli powder, ¼ teaspoon turmeric and a pinch of salt and rub over the fish steaks. Set aside.

Wash, peel and cut the potatoes into quarters and mix them with ¼ teaspoon chilli powder and ¼ teaspoon turmeric. Mix well. Rub ¼ teaspoon chilli powder and a pinch of salt into the cauliflower florets and set aside.

In a spice mill mix the ginger and cumin seeds with just enough water to make a paste.

Heat the oil in a wok or large pan and add the cauliflower florets. Cook for 2–3 minutes, then drain on kitchen paper. Add the potatoes to the wok and cook until lightly golden then remove and drain in the same way. Finally shallow-fry the fish for a few minutes, drain and set aside.

To the same oil (if you feel there is too much remove a couple of spoonfuls), add the bay leaves, green cardamom pods, cinnamon stick and cloves and allow to infuse. Add the onion seeds and allow them to crackle. Once crackled add the ginger cumin paste and cook for 2 minutes.

Add the remaining chilli powder, turmeric and salt together with the coriander. Mix well. Add 2 cups of water and bring to the boil.

Add the cauliflower florets, potatoes and fish, reduce the heat and simmer gently for 10 minutes.

Adjust the seasoning, squeeze over the lemon and serve hot with steamed rice.

GHANTE

Bengali vegetable curry

SERVES 4

6 baby aubergines

2 medium potatoes

150 g/5½ oz pumpkin

2 green (unripe) bananas

150 g/5½ oz runner beans

6 parwal (gourd)

3 tablespoons mustard oil

2 green chillies, slit
lengthways in half

2 dried red chillies

1 teaspoon ground coriander

1 teaspoon chilli powder

1 teaspoon ground turmeric

½ teaspoon ground cumin

salt, to taste

few sprigs chopped fresh
coriander

Cut the aubergines into 2-cm/¾-inch round slices. Peel the potatoes, pumpkin and parwal and cut into 2-cm/¾-inch pieces. Peel the bananas and cut into 2-cm/¾-inch pieces. String the beans and cut into 2.5-cm/1-inch pieces. Peel and cut the parwal into 2-cm/¾-inch pieces.

Wash all the cut vegetables and pat dry with kitchen paper.

Heat the oil in a non-stick pan and fry the green chillies and dried red chillies for 30 seconds.

Add all the vegetables together and fry them till a golden crust starts to show around them. Add the ground coriander, chilli powder, turmeric and cumin.

Add 2–3 tablespoons water and salt to taste. Cover the pan and cook over a low heat for about 5 minutes until until the vegetables are just done.

Sprinkle with chopped fresh coriander and serve with steamed rice.

Note This makes a great accompaniment to Mustard fish and mango curry (see page 50).

PATUREE

Prawn and crab cakes

SERVES 4

200 g/7 oz prawns, peeled and deveined

200 g/7 oz white crabmeat

1 medium potato, peeled, cooked and grated

few curry leaves, chopped

few sprigs fresh coriander, chopped

3 tablespoons mustard oil

30 g/1¼ oz grated Cheddar cheese

¾ teaspoon ground turmeric

1 teaspoon chilli powder

1 teaspoon garam masala

½ teaspoon dried chilli flakes

salt, to taste

juice of 1 lemon

2 banana leaves

Mint and coriander chutney (see page 133), to serve

Wash the prawns, drain in a colander and roughly chop.

Mix together the chopped prawns, crabmeat, potato, curry leaves, fresh coriander, mustard oil, cheese, ground turmeric, chilli powder, garam masala, dried chilli flakes and salt and mix well. Pour over the lemon juice.

Wipe each banana leaf with a damp cloth and then trim and cut each one into six pieces.

Divide the mixture into 12 and shape into patties. Wrap each one in a piece of banana leaf, making sure that the filling does not come out.

Heat a non-stick pan, sear the wrapped leaves then cook for 4–5 minutes on each side. Serve with Mint and coriander chutney.

CALCUTTA

SO IT BEGINS. Calcutta, Bengal. All the way over on the flight I found myself intermittently humming the Punjabi folk song, GT Road. (That and "Flying Without Wings" by Westlife; no doubt caused by some bizarre Freudian fear of flying lodged in my subconscious.) The irony is that I couldn't be further from the Punjab, the object of the desire of that folk song, than when arriving in Bengal.

Amritsar is 1,153 miles away; a journey stretching over numerous states of India into Pakistan and beyond to Kabul. I have been to Calcutta once before and have strong, visceral memories of the city. It is a myriad of mayhem, a panoply of pandemonium; unsurprising given that it is calculated to be the world's eighth largest urban agglomeration. (I don't really know what that means but I reckon Calcutta must be one of the most densely populated cities in the world.) Mayhem and pandemonium.

My childhood memories of Calcutta were mostly about talk of how cultured the Bengalis were. They have served India disproportionately well in terms of the Arts and Culture and the state is very much defined by its passion for politics. Since the 1970s West Bengal has been ruled by Marxists; and the Left appears to be holding up even in the face of the free market flood that has transformed the rest of the nation.

I suppose what defines modern-day Calcutta more than anything is the city's role in the evolution of the Raj. The East India Company set up shop there in 1690 and the port town soon became a strategically important city to the colonialists, being adopted as the Capital of the British Empire in India until 1911. Fascinatingly, the city was split in the 1850s into White Town and Black Town... the names need no further explanation. The Raj brought the Chinese in to work in the docks and surrounding industries. It seems to have always been a cosmopolitan city, combining the usual unusualness of any major port city with the influence of the British.

And while Ani's soul maybe be from the beating heart of the Punjab, his very heart belongs to Calcutta. He fell in love with a Bengali girl, a love no doubt fuelled by food. It's going to be interesting to see if the food of Bengal has a similarly aphrodisiacal effect on me!

My first port of call, food-wise, is to Calcutta's Chinatown. For years I have been obsessive about exploring Britain's Chinese food and dim sum in particular; an obsession my Indian cousins share with me. Whilst we Brits go for beer and curry on a Friday, middle-class Indians like nothing better than a Chinese meal, obviously spiced up to suit a different palate. I know Calcutta has one of the world's

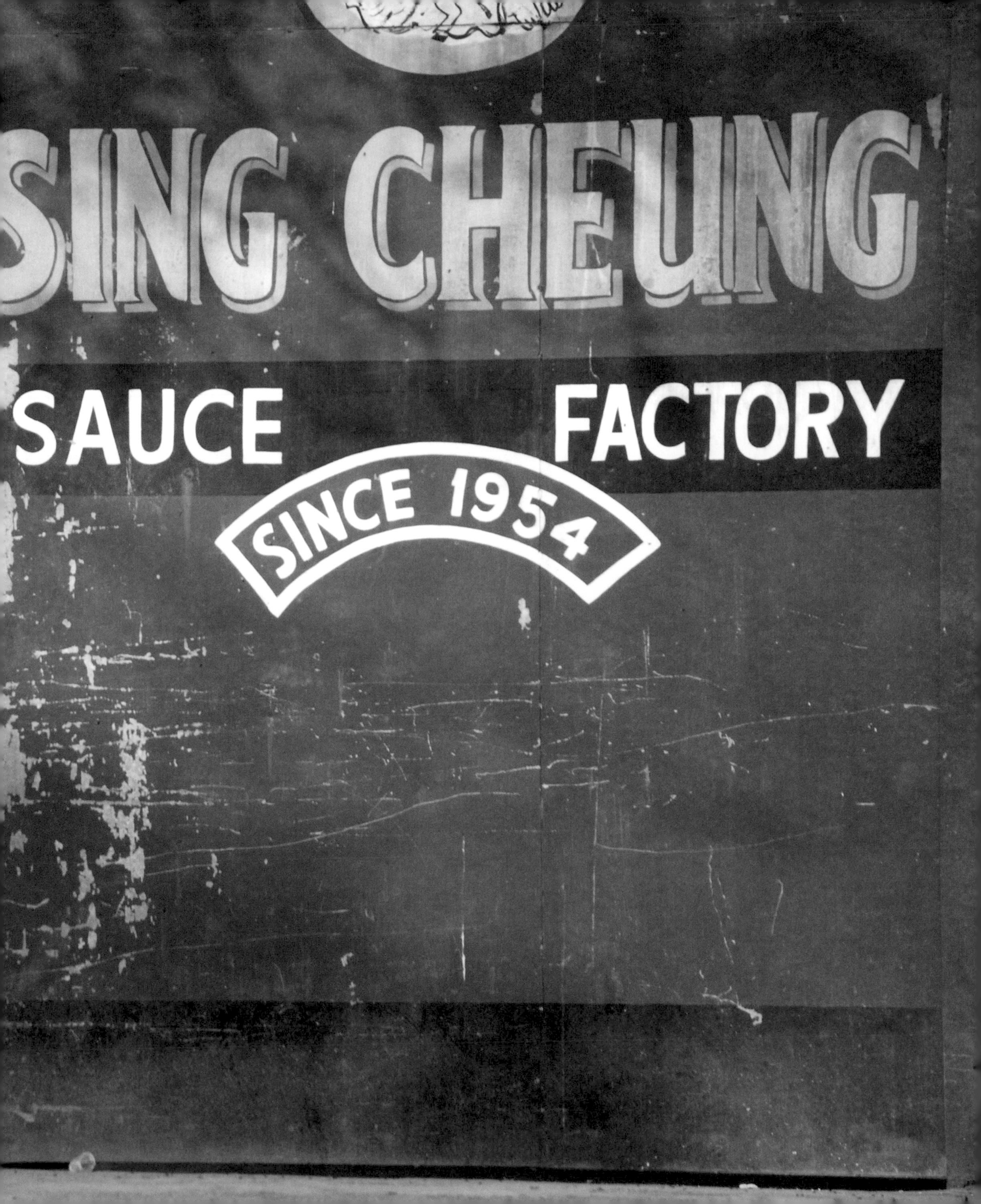
SING CHEUNG
SAUCE FACTORY
SINCE 1954

oldest Chinatowns and I have had the hunger to eat there for years. Luckily for me, it sits close to the start of the GT Road so it is both a duty and a pleasure.

The Chinese made their name in the city as leather makers, a trade usually left to the lower caste Indians, Chamars. Their tanneries and workshops were spread out in the heart of the city until some ten years ago when they were uprooted from the city centre and moved out to an area called Tangra. The area is still a hive of activity; cafes and restaurants sit cheek-by-jowl with small shops and leather sellers. Walking through the streets I can smell the unmistakable aroma of Chinese food from every corner. Choice-wise, I'm spoilt. There is also a definite air of faded glory about the place, a palpable sadness in the air. The break up of the Chinese tannery businesses led to the fragmenting of the Chinese community in Calcutta. It is reckoned that as many as 80 percent of the Chinese community moved away, taking with them their history and traditions.

A place called Golden Joy has been recommended by a local and luckily enough the owner, Edwin, is around. While I wait for my dumplings we chat a little and he tells me that he thinks Calcutta is still the best place in the world to celebrate Chinese New Year. Apparently loads of those Chinese that have left return to celebrate.

Edwin tells me that the people of Calcutta are always talking about food. Constantly. Restaurants originally started in people's houses and front rooms, all you needed was a few tables and some home-cooked food. These necessarily developed into cafes and restaurants — yet still there is a feeling in Tangra of casual, homely eating. While Edwin talks I tuck in to an enormous plate of siu mai dumplings. Siu mai is, for me, the basic Chinese dim sum — delicious and flavourful. I always say that the best way to judge the quality of dim sum in any restaurant is to first order the siu mai. If they are good then order the rest of the meal. Yet these siu mai, while good, are uniquely different. The normal marriage of pork and prawn has not been blessed. These are chicken and prawn, in deference to the small but important Muslim community in the city. Pork is rare to find in India outside Goa, the predominantly Christian state.

I finish my dumplings and wander off to find another place to nibble, such is the delight of dim sum. I can't help but feel the Marxist influence in Calcutta amongst the Chinese residences, particularly when I come across a bright red mural of a hammer and sickle on one of the white walls, below which an older Chinese man sits with his feet up on a similarly Marxist-red plastic footstool while a younger gent drags suspiciously on a cigarette.

Edwin suggested we find a place called Kim Fa for honest-to-goodness Chinese food. 'Nothing fancy' he said as he sent us looking for the Chinese Kala Mandir, the Black Temple; Kim Fa is adjacent to the Mandir. There was certainly 'nothing fancy' about the place, which consisted of five tables and a cold concrete floor. I ordered Ginger Fish, bhekti, a freshwater river fish from the Mama Ganga. It was basically a fish pakora emboldened by fresh ginger in the batter; delicious but not very Chinese. The fish was like bream, the gingery batter light and crisp. Quite the opposite of how I feel after consuming my bodyweight in lunchtime Chinese delights!

Like so many Indian cities, Calcutta transforms under the canopy of darkness. The bustle and the hustle seem to find new extremes as the gloom of night ensues. As the light fades I glide through the streets, a man on a mission, a very specific mission. A Kathi Roll mission. In a small turning off the main drag, Park Road, there's a place called Kusum's Rolls and Kebabs. Evening has most definitely fallen with a graceless bump, and the cacophony of the city finds its own discordant rhythm. Kusum's is doing a roaring trade. And they specialise in kathi roll. Such is the memory of kathi roll that whenever it is mentioned in front of Ani his eyes well up and he looks off into the middle distance. It's very similar to his reaction when he talks about meeting his wife. The kathi roll I am here to try is filled with mutton.

The hut itself is just two men deep and no more than thirteen feet wide, hewn into the side of a building. Behind the counter three bodies move and work and cook. A man takes orders and money; a boy/man fills the rolls and a third fella makes the bread or paratha. On the customer side of the hut a 12-year-old boy rolls large discs of flour dough to an almost uniform diameter of seven inches. These are lightly oiled and then placed on a massive tava, a flat steel plate big enough to accommodate at least thirty of these doughy discs. Expertly, the third fella fries the parathas to a crisp golden-brown, ever-aware of which requires turning at any specific moment. The cooked breads are then passed to the boy/man to be stuffed and finally to the customer to be consumed. It is a beautiful process to behold: four sets of hands hurrying to create. In a quarter of an hour I witnessed almost four dozen rolls despatched. They sell around a thousand kathi rolls a day. That's a third of a million a year. Unfortunately today they are not serving mutton, but there is no shortage of available fillings.

At first my eye has been caught by an egg version of the roll, reminding me of a classic Punjabi breakfast dish of Aanda ka Paratha, egg-stuffed paratha. Whereas the Punjabi version is straightforward stodge, the Bengali kathi has some twists and turns. An egg is broken on the almost cooked paratha, and scrambled. The cooked egg/paratha is then stuffed with onions, freshly chopped green chillies and (bizarrely) Chinese spiced tomato sauce.

I've decided to order two kathi rolls: single egg and double chicken. Chicken and egg. I wonder which will come first?

They were utterly delicious. Surprisingly light for what one might expect to be a ponderously heavy snack, given the frying process. And neither were they overly spiced. I enjoyed the most delightful silence in my own head as I consumed one after the other. Taking a moment to capture an image of the busy hut and the never-diminishing queue of hungry customers, I slip off into the Calcutta gloom for a couple of vodka tonics. But, like all truly great food, the memory never remains too distant. I returned after my third vodka for a double egg kathi roll.

The next day I venture out to College Road, a street lined with second-hand bookshop after second-hand bookshop. Piles of books everywhere, a vista of spines faces you in every direction. In amongst this library of leaning and learning, up some stairs overlooking the street below is the Marxist Coffee Shop. (It isn't actually named 'The Marxist Coffee Shop' but all the locals refer to it thus). The India Coffee House is single room and balcony and has a decidedly colonial feel; it's light and bright and breezy. The staff, all men of mid-age and beyond, wear once-white uniforms and turbans.

Missing my mutton kathi roll from the night before, I order a mutton sandwich and a coffee. The sandwich bread is that slightly sweet Indian-style bread that I know and don't quite love. Unbuttered it requires more than the usual amount of peristalsis to send the mouthful stomach-ward. The coffee is delicious, freshly filtered and served in dainty little white coffee cups. This is a late-morning snack since lunch is to be at a place called Kewpies. If eating were an Olympic sport I reckon I could be team captain.

Kewpies seems to be a bit of an institution in these parts. Ani insisted I visit and eat. I was expecting a huge, expansive restaurant bustling with life and food, similar to Moti Mahal. Instead the intense red exterior hides nothing more than a residential house that has been fashioned into a small 50-cover restaurant. It's a charming place with the lady of the house at the helm in the kitchen, a classic Bengali matriarch.

We sip on a salty sweet mango drink. The menu is all about the auryvedic principles of five flavours: salt, spice, astringent, sour and bitter. And the flavours are subtle, unlike the heavyweight Punjabi food that awaits me at the other end of my journey.

We are starting with Chingri Maacher Chiney Kebab, the Bengali take on lobster thermidor. The 'Chiney' reference is fascinating. Anything foreign to Bengal is referred to as 'Chiney' or Chinese. We are then having a thali, with a selection of dishes. We have also ordered Duck Vindaloo (a Portuguese dish brought to Bengal in colonial days), Smoked Hilsa, an Anglo-Indian dish of smoked, deboned fish with an anchovy sauce. And finally, Ani's favourite, Chingri Malai, prawns in a creamy sauce. This promises to be quintessentially Bengali food, served in a homely fashion. The Chingri Malai is as creamy as promised with a prominent flavour of cloves and coconut and a back flavour of the deliciously astringent tamarind. A delicately textured dish that dances a tango across the palate. I have to confess to feeling more than a little surprised at the subtlety of authentic Bengali food.

The Howrah Bridge that crosses the Ganga is the modern route out of Calcutta heading West on the GT Road to Kabul. Three lanes in both directions, full of traffic. Ideally I would travel by road out of Bengal into the neighbouring state of Bihar. Bihar was once, like Bengal, a place of great culture and learning. The ancient and greatest of all Indian empires, the Mauryan empire, originated from modern-day Bihar over two millennia ago. But that was two millennia ago. The truth of modern day Bihar is that it had become a fairly lawless state, highwaymen roaming roads, shotgun law and brutal violence. And while there has been a definite turnaround in the fortunes of the state it was still regarded as too dangerous to drive through.

By way of allowance I eat at a dhaba a few miles from the Bihar state border. Shere-e-Bengal dhaba is simply a concrete shack with no more than twenty seats, simple wooden tables and plastic chairs. A lone chef fries and cooks and chats as the sun conspires to set. The basic accommodation of this street café is embellished by a small fish tank with a few sorry looking goldfish. One can't help but wonder their fate... A chai wallah is making tea while limes are squeezed. Chana is soaking in preparation for tomorrow's lunch and nestling next to them an enormous bag of chillies, more than a dozen mooli and half a dozen bunches of fresh coriander. So many flavours yet to be concocted.

The menu is simple: Mutton Curry, Anda Bhurji (egg curry), Kali Dal (black lentils), Fish and Egg Curry, Palak Paneer (fenugreek and Indian cheese), Fish Fry. Three simple coal burners for the cooking and plenty of Hindi music. An ever-changing army of Tata trucks stop and leave, hungry diners enjoy the utilitarian food with no small sense of bonhomie. The food is rustic and hearty; drivers' food, frill-free.

Shere-e-Bengal dhaba sits at the head of the modern GT Road. I leave there to find the original GT Road, the one that prevailed before the Howrah bridge opened. I am 17 km from the city in an area called Dhankoni. Dhabas to the left of me, dhabas to the right, here I am, stuck in the middle with you. The old GT road is but two lanes; they run alongside a six-lane highway. Small shanty towns line the way, families feed in their open-air lives. Rows of washed clothes hang on lines, demarcating one space, one home from another... walls made of freshly washed fabric.

The road hugs the line of the River Ganga, no further than a shack's depth away. The densely packed narrow road with little gullies of surprise, alleys full of secrets. There is nothing grand or trunk-like about this road as it bobs and weaves its way into Calcutta city.

On this ancient, now forlorn GT Road I come across Litte Wallah Chai Bandah. Cross-legged he sits, a modern day deity of the tea leaf. His white-vested body, his pink-dhoti'd legs sit crossed underneath him. His intensely black back-swept hair continues into an intensely black long beard both of which match the intensity of his black brown eyes. He is intense. His stall, no more than 5 ft by 4 ft, is almost half given over to a garlanded shrine behind him. Around him he is hemmed in by hills of clay cups, pinkish in hue. Tea making is worship for this Litte Wallah Chai bandah. He doesn't make tea; no. He creates tea, he crafts tea, he conjures tea. There is so much complexity in the making of what would appear a simple cup of tea. The pot is banged and soothed. The heat is calmed and encouraged. The tea is spiced and served. There is theatre in his tea, drama in his tea and as I sip a cup I hope there will be no tragedy in his tea. The tea is flavoured with rose water... the milky, malty mixture is as perfect as tea can be. As I sip my tea I eat Litte, a road-side snack that is favoured by the poorest traveller. A small dough ball that has been griddled. It is filled with spiced chickpea, served on a small plate with a coriander and mustard oil chutney and a spiced potato sabhzi. This is food for the very poorest folk; they may be poor, but their food is rich in flavour. I stay for another cup, another ceremony. Tomorrow I leave the east and head west.

KATHI ROLL

Chicken wraps

SERVES 4

FOR THE FILLING

3 tablespoons vegetable oil

½ teaspoon cumin seeds

3 onions, sliced

I tablespoon ginger and garlic paste (see page 30)

I teaspoon chilli powder

I teaspoon ground coriander

¼ teaspoon ground turmeric

salt, to taste

500 g/I lb 2 oz boneless chicken thighs, cut into 2-cm/¾-inch pieces

2 tomatoes, chopped

½ teaspoon garam masala

I tablespoon chopped fresh coriander

FOR THE PARATHAS

750 g/I lb 10 oz plain flour

salt, to taste

2 tablespoons oil, plus extra for cooking

water, to knead

4 eggs, beaten

2.5-cm/I-inch piece ginger, peeled and cut into julienne

chopped fresh coriander

chilli sauce (optional)

First make the filling. Heat the oil in a large pan, add the cumin seeds and allow them to crackle. Add half of the sliced onion and cook until golden brown.

Add the ginger and garlic paste and cook for 2 minutes. Add the chilli powder, ground coriander, turmeric and salt. Mix well.

Add the diced chicken and sear on all sides. Add the chopped tomatoes and cook until soft. Add ½ cup water and cook over a medium heat until the chicken is tender and all the liquid has evaporated. Sprinkle over the garam masala and chopped fresh coriander and set aside.

To make the parathas, mix the flour, salt and oil in a large bowl. Make a well in the centre and add enough water to make a soft dough, about 150–200 ml (5–7 fl oz). Cover with a damp cloth and set aside for 30 minutes.

Divide the dough into four pieces and roll each one out into thin flat breads like tortilla.

Heat a non-stick pan or a flat griddle pan, place the paratha on the hot pan and spread I teaspoon oil on one side. Flip the paratha over, brush generously with beaten egg and cook. Turn the paratha and repeat on the other side. Repeat with the other parathas.

To assemble the rolls: lay an egg paratha on a clean flat surface, add 2 tablespoons of the chicken mixture in a line, down the centre of the paratha. Place the remaining sliced onion, ginger strips, chopped fresh coriander and chilli sauce, if using, on top and roll the paratha tightly to a wrap.

Baigun Bhaja

Fried aubergines

SERVES 4

2 large aubergines

1 teaspoon ground turmeric

1 teaspoon chilli powder

salt, to taste

4 tablespoons mustard or vegetable oil

Slice the aubergines into discs, about 2-cm/¾-inch thick.

Mix together the ground turmeric, chilli powder and salt and rub the aubergine slices with the spice mix.

Heat the oil in a large non-stick frying pan and add the aubergine slices a few at a time. Reduce the heat and cook the slices for 1½ minutes on each side, or until golden brown. Drain on kitchen paper and serve hot.

Lau Kosher Chhechki

Gourd and potato stir-fry

SERVES 4

2 medium potatoes

peel of 1 lauki (gourd), sliced
into 5-cm/2-inch pieces

3 tablespoons mustard oil

50 g/1¾ oz Bengali vadi
(lentil dumplings)

1 teaspoon black mustard
seeds

2 teaspoons poppy seeds

3 green chillies, slit
lengthways

salt, to taste

½ teaspoon ground turmeric

juice of 1 lemon

few sprigs fresh coriander,
chopped

Slice the potatoes into 2.5-cm/1-inch slices and set aside with the lauki peel.

Heat 2 tablespoons of mustard oil and fry the vadi till golden brown, drain on kitchen paper and set aside.

Heat the remaining mustard oil, add the mustard and poppy seeds and allow them to crackle. Add the green chillies, the gourd skin and potato slices and cook for 5–6 minutes.

Add salt and turmeric. Cover and cook over a low heat until the vegetables are fully cooked, about 5–6 minutes. Mix in the vadi and turn off the heat. (Do overmix as the vadi will break up.)

Add the lemon juice and sprinkle with chopped fresh coriander.

Note In a Bengali meal this dish would be served as a starter with steamed rice, followed by the meat or fish dish.

Kumro Phool Bhaja

Stuffed courgette flowers

SERVES 4

8 courgette flowers

FOR THE BATTER
100 g/3½ oz chickpea flour
50 g/1¾ oz tempura flour
1 teaspoon chilli powder
½ teaspoon ground turmeric
2.5-cm/1-inch piece ginger, peeled and finely grated
2 red chillies, chopped
few curry leaves, chopped
few sprigs fresh coriander, chopped
½ teaspoon garam masala
salt, to taste
juice of 1 lemon
water, as required

FOR THE FILLING
1 medium potato, peeled and cooked
2 skinless whiting fillets, pin-boned
½ teaspoon ground turmeric
¼ teaspoon chilli powder
¼ teaspoon dried chilli flakes
¼ teaspoon garam masala
few sprigs fresh coriander, chopped
2.5-cm/1-inch piece ginger, peeled and finely grated
2 green chillies, chopped
salt, to taste
juice of ½ lemon
1 tablespoon mustard oil
20 g/¾ oz Cheddar cheese, grated
1 teaspoon cornflour

First make the batter. Put the chickpea flour, tempura flour, chilli powder, turmeric, ginger, red chillies, curry leaves, fresh coriander, garam masala and salt in a bowl. Mix well.

Add the lemon juice. Pour in enough water to make a smooth thin batter and mix well.

To make the filling, grate the potato and set aside. Poach the fish in water for 5–6 minutes, drain, cool and set aside.

In a large mixing bowl, add the fish, grated potato, ground turmeric, chilli powder, dried chilli flakes, garam masala, coriander, ginger, green chilli and salt. Mix well.

Add the lemon juice. Add mustard oil, grated cheese and cornflour and mix well. Check for seasoning.

Cut the stalks off the courgette flowers and carefully stuff them with the fish mixture, folding the ends under carefully to hold in the mixture.

Dredge the stuffed flowers in 1 tablespoons tempura flour then dip them in batter (make sure all the extra batter drips off) and deep-fry over a medium heat until golden brown and crisp.

Serve hot with Date and tomato and chutney (see page 54).

Shorshey Macch

Mustard fish and mango curry

SERVES 4

4 fish steaks (eg sea bass, sea bream, carp or red snapper)

³/₄ teaspoon ground turmeric

1¹/₂ teaspoons chilli powder

salt, to taste

oil, for frying

50 g/1³/₄ oz yellow mustard seeds

4 green chillies, slit lengthways

6 tablespoons mustard oil

2 tomatoes, roughly chopped

1 teaspoon onion seeds

¹/₂ green mango, sliced

¹/₂ teaspoon ground cumin

few sprigs fresh coriander, chopped

Wash the fish. Drain and pat dry. Rub ¹/₄ teaspoon ground turmeric, ¹/₂ teaspoon chilli powder and a pinch of salt into the fish.

Heat the oil in a wok and add the fish steaks one at a time and fry over a medium heat until crisp and golden brown. Drain on kitchen paper and set aside.

Soak the mustard seeds in ¹/₄ cup of water for 30 minutes. Place 2 green chillies, 3 tablespoons of mustard oil and the soaked mustard seeds in a spice mill or small blender. Grind or blend until you have a smooth paste. Set aside.

Put the tomatoes in a food processor or blender and process briefly. Set aside.

Heat the remaining mustard oil in a pan, add onion seeds and allow them to crackle. Once they crackle, add the remaining green chillies and mustard paste. Cook for 5–6 minutes over a low heat until the oil separates.

Add the tomatoes, the remaining turmeric and chilli powder and season to taste. Cook for 3–4 minutes.

Add the sliced mango and cook for a minute or until soft. Add enough water to cover and allow it to simmer for 5–6 minutes. Add the fried fish and cook for 5–6 minutes.

Turn off the heat and add ground cumin and chopped fresh coriander.

CHINGRI MALAI

Prawns with coconut

SERVES 4

3 green fresh coconuts

2 green chillies, slit
lengthways

2 teaspoons poppy seeds,
mixed with water in a mill
and reduced to a fine paste

600 g/1 lb 5 oz large raw
shell-on prawns

1½ tablespoons oil

salt, to taste

lemon wedges, to serve

Cut open the coconuts and, reserving the sweet coconut water, cut
the flesh into chunks. Blend the soft flesh with a little water to obtain
a smooth purée. Add 1 green chilli to this and cook over a low heat
in a pan till it boils. Add the poppy seed paste and boil for a further
2–3 minutes. Set aside.

Wash the prawns, drain and pat dry. Carefully remove the heads and
shell, leaving the tails intact. Pour the oil into a pan, add the
remaining green chilli and the prawns and sauté for a few seconds.
Add the coconut water and cook for 2–3 minutes, depending on the
size of the prawns.

Add the coconut and poppy seed paste to the prawns and cook for
a further 2 minutes, until the sauce starts to thicken.

Season to taste and serve with lemon wedges.

Tamatar Khejoorer Chutney

Date and tomato chutney

SERVES 4

12 dates, stoned

3 tablespoons vegetable oil

1 teaspoon mustard seeds

3 dried red chillies

few curry leaves

2.5-cm/1-inch piece ginger, peeled and finely chopped

10 tomatoes, skinned, deseeded and chopped

1 teaspoon chilli powder

½ teaspoon ground cumin

½ teaspoon black peppercorns, crushed

50 g/1¾ oz jaggery, grated

3 tablespoons white vinegar

salt, to taste

Soak the dates in warm water for 10 minutes, then drain and chop roughly. Set aside.

Heat the oil in a pan then add the mustard seeds and allow them to crackle. Once crackled add the dried chillies, curry leaves and chopped ginger and cook for about 30 seconds.

Add the chopped tomatoes, chilli powder, cumin, crushed black peppercorns, salt to taste and mix well. Cover and cook for about 5 minutes until the tomatoes soften.

Add the jaggery and the chopped dates and cook for 10 minutes, until the mixture turns to pulp and thickens. Add the white vinegar and cook for 2 minutes.

Turn off the heat and leave to cool. Serve cold with Stuffed courgette flowers (see page 49).

CHOKHA

Spiced aubergine mash

SERVES 4

2 large aubergines

3 tomatoes

2.5-cm/1-inch piece ginger, peeled and chopped

3 green chillies, chopped

few sprigs fresh coriander, chopped

2 tablespoons mustard oil

1/2 teaspoon cumin seeds

4 dried red chillies

1/4 teaspoon ground turmeric

1/2 teaspoon chilli powder

salt, to taste

juice of 1 lemon

Roast the aubergines and tomatoes separately by placing them under a hot grill for about 10 minutes and turning until the skins are lightly charred on all sides. Cool, skin and mash together.

Mix the ginger, green chillies and fresh coriander in a bowl and add to the aubergine and tomato.

Heat the oil in a pan, add the cumin seeds and allow them to crackle. Once crackled, add the dried red chillies, turmeric and chilli powder and cook for 1–2 minutes. Allow to cool.

Add the spiced oil to the aubergine and tomato mash and mix well. Adjust the seasoning and pour over the lemon juice. Serve cold.

Achari Baigan

Baby aubergine cooked with pickling spices

SERVES 4

4 tomatoes, roughly chopped

10 long baby aubergines

60 ml/2 fl oz vegetable oil

½ teaspoon panch phoran
(see page 210)

3 green chillies, slit
lengthways

2 onions, very finely chopped

I teaspoon chilli powder

I teaspoon ground coriander

½ teaspoon ground turmeric

salt, to taste

30 g/I oz jaggery, grated

juice of I lemon

few sprigs fresh coriander,
chopped

2.5-cm/I-inch piece ginger,
peeled and cut into julienne

FOR THE MASALA

I tablespoon chilli powder

2 tablespoons ground
coriander

I tablespoon ground cumin

I tablespoon amchoor (dried
mango powder)

I teaspoon garam masala

salt, to taste

I tablespoon panch phoran,
crushed (see page 210)

First make the masala. Put all the masala ingredients in a bowl and mix well. Set aside.

Put the tomatoes in a food processor or blender and process until you have a smooth purée. Slice the aubergines lengthways but do not cut them all the way through. Rub the inside of each aubergine with ½ teaspoon of the masala (the rest can be stored for several weeks in an airtight container).

Heat half the oil in a non-stick pan and fry the aubergines over a low heat, turning regularly, until three quarters cooked. Drain on kitchen paper and set aside.

Heat the remaining oil in a pan, add the panch phoran and allow it to crackle. Once crackled add the green chillies and sauté. Add the onions and cook until golden brown. Add the chilli powder, ground coriander, turmeric and salt. Mix well.

Add the puréed tomatoes and cook until the oil separates and thickens. Add the fried aubergines and cook over a medium heat until soft, about 5 minutes. Sprinkle over a few tablespoons of water if you feel the mixture is too dry. Add the grated jaggery and mix until dissolved.

Pour over the lemon juice and sprinkle over the chopped fresh coriander, ginger julienne and a tablespoon of the masala.

ALOO PURI

Potato curry with deep-fried bread

SERVES 4

FOR THE PURI

400 g/14 oz wholemeal flour

salt, to taste

2 tablespoons vegetable oil

cold water, to knead

vegetable oil, for deep-frying

FOR THE POTATO CURRY

4 medium potatoes

6 tomatoes

2–3 tablespoons vegetable oil

1/2 teaspoon cumin seeds

2.5-cm/1-inch piece ginger, peeled and chopped

2 green chillies, chopped

1/4 teaspoon asafoetida

1/2 teaspoon ground turmeric

I teaspoon chilli powder

I teaspoon ground coriander

salt, to taste

juice of I lemon

I teaspoon garam masala

few sprigs fresh coriander, chopped

First make the dough for the puri. Mix the flour, salt and oil in a bowl. Make a well in the centre and add enough water to make a smooth but firm dough. Cover with a damp cloth and set aside for 30 minutes.

Boil the whole potatoes in their skins. Once they are just cooked, skin them and mash roughly, with bite-sized pieces of potato left in the mash. Blend the tomatoes to a smooth purée in a food processor. Set aside.

Heat the oil in a pan, add the cumin seeds and allow them to crackle. Add the ginger, chopped green chillies and asafoetida and sauté for a couple of seconds. Add about 2–3 teaspoons water to stop the pan from catching.

Stir in the turmeric, chilli powder, ground coriander and salt. Add the puréed tomatoes and cook for 7–8 minutes until the sauce starts to thicken. Add the mashed potatoes and stir through. Cover and cook for 2 minutes. Add about 1½ cups of water and cook for 4–5 minutes.

Meanwhile, divide the dough equally into about 12–16 balls. On an oiled surface roll each ball into a thin circle, 8–10 cm (3–4 inches) in diameter.

Heat the oil in a wok and add the puri one at a time. Deep-fry for a few seconds on each side until puffed and golden. Drain on kitchen paper and keep warm.

Remove the potato curry from the heat, pour over the lemon juice and sprinkle with garam masala and chopped fresh coriander. Serve the potato curry with hot puri.

GULKAND KA PEDA

Rose petal rolls

SERVES 4

2 tablespoons gulkand

360 g/12¼ oz icing sugar, sifted

500 g/1 lb 2 oz khoya, grated

½ teaspoon ground cardamom

silver leaf, to decorate

chopped pistachio nuts, to decorate

Heat a non-stick pan, add the gulkand and cook for 5 minutes over a low heat until dry. Turn off the heat and set aside to cool.

Mix together the icing sugar and grated khoya thoroughly in a bowl. Place another non-stick pan over the heat, add the sugar and khoya and cook over a low heat until the mixture is thick and starts to form a soft ball.

Stir in the ground cardamom and then transfer to a clean bowl and set aside to cool.

To make the rolls, divide the mixture into equal-sized pieces, about the size of a walnut. Flatten each piece in the palm of your hand and then place ¼ teaspoon gulkand mixture in the centre.

Now roll the khoya gently so that the gulkand is covered by the mixture and it does not come out.

Wrap each individual roll with silver leaf and decorate with pistachios.

PARWAL KI MITHAI

Sweet parwal filled with khoya

SERVES 4

250 g/9 oz khoya

400 g/14 oz caster sugar

¼ teaspoon ground green cardamom

15 almonds, chopped

15 pistachios, chopped

300 ml/½ pint water

500 g/1 lb 2 oz parwal (gourd)

pinch of bicarbonate of soda

silver leaf, to decorate

few strands saffron, to decorate

Place the khoya in a non-stick pan over a medium to low heat until soft. Add 100 g/3½ oz of caster sugar and cook for 8–10 minutes, stirring regularly.

Add the ground green cardamom and mix well. Turn off the heat and add the chopped almonds and pistachios. Mix well and then transfer the filling to a clean bowl and set aside to cool.

In a small heavy-based pan, dissolve the remaining sugar in the water and allow it to boil to make a thin sugar syrup.

Peel and slit the parwal lengthways. Do not cut through. Deseed and set aside.

Bring a large pan of water to the boil and add to this the bicarbonate of soda. Add the parwal to the boiling water and cook for 4–5 minutes or until it almost soft.

Drain and add the parwal to the sugar syrup and simmer for 2–3 minutes until soft. Remove from the syrup and set aside to cool.

Stuff the parwal with the khoya mixture and decorate it with silver leaf and saffron strands.

GAZAK

Peanut and pistachio brittle

SERVES 4

30 g/1¼ oz sesame seeds

150 g/5½ oz peanuts, skinned

150 g/5½ oz caster sugar

3 tablespoons vegetable oil, plus extra for greasing

250 g/9 oz jaggery, grated

30 g/1¼ oz pistachios

Toast the sesame seeds in a non-stick frying pan over a low heat until golden brown. Toast the peanuts in the same way until golden brown. Set aside.

Place the sugar in a small heavy-based pan and cook over a low heat until it melts and turns to a light golden caramel.

Heat the oil in a non-stick pan and add grated jaggery and cook over a low heat for 4–6 minutes, stirring continuously. Mix in the caramelized sugar.

Take the pan off the heat and stir in the peanuts, sesame seeds and pistachios. Mix well.

Lightly grease a baking tray with oil and spoon the mixture onto it, smoothing it with a palette knife until even.

Once the mixture starts to set, cut into the desired shapes and allow to cool.

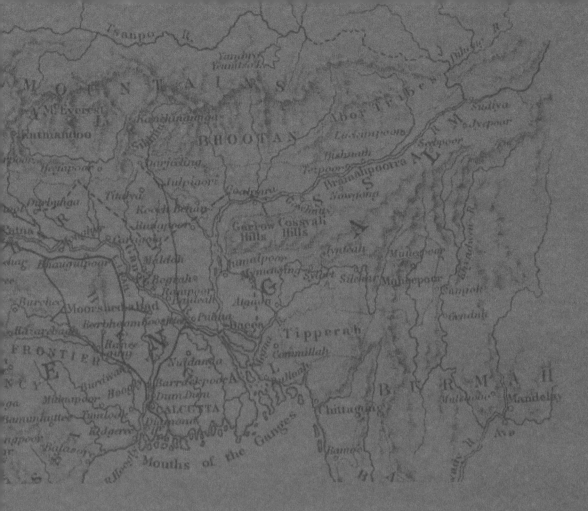

Uttar Pradesh

Uttar Pradesh is a melting pot of Awadhi Muslim culture, Mughal history and die-hard Hindu brahmnical order. The region's economy is agriculture based. The cultural hot spots are Benares, Allahabad, Agra and Lucknow. The aristocratic and fine-tuned Awadhi cuisine features delicate kebabs, kormas, biriyanis and shallow-fried breads. The Ghats of Benares are famous for their simple but delicately flavoured vegetarian dishes and sweets based on thickened milk and fried wheat dough recipes. Ghee is used in dishes throughout the state.

DAL KACHORI

Deep-fried bread filled with spiced lentils

SERVES 4

FOR THE DOUGH

300 g/11 oz plain flour

salt, to taste

3 tablespoons vegetable oil, plus extra for deep-frying

cold water, to knead

FOR THE FILLING

180 g/6 oz moong dal (yellow lentils)

vegetable oil, for frying

1/2 teaspoon fennel seeds

1/2 teaspoon cumin seeds

1/4 teaspoon asafoetida

2.5-cm/1-inch piece ginger, peeled and chopped

3 green chillies, chopped

1 teaspoon chilli powder

1/4 teaspoon ground turmeric

salt, to taste

1 teaspoon ground coriander

1 tablespoon amchoor (dried mango powder)

few sprigs fresh coriander, chopped

juice of 1 lemon

1 teaspoon garam masala

Tamarind chutney (see page 132), to serve

First make the dough. Mix the flour, salt and oil in a bowl. Make a well in the centre and add enough water to make a tight or hard dough. Cover with a damp cloth and set aside to rest for 30 minutes.

Make the filling. Wash and soak the lentils for 30 minutes. Drain and set aside. Put the lentils in a saucepan, add enough water to cover and bring to the boil. Cook for 3–4 minutes, then drain, refresh under cold water and drain again. Set aside.

Heat the oil in a pan, add the fennel and cumin seeds and allow them to crackle then add the asafoetida, chopped ginger and green chilli and sauté for 2 minutes. Add the cooked lentils and sauté for 2 minutes. Add the chilli powder, turmeric, salt and ground coriander and cook for 2–3 minutes. Mix well but do not mash the lentils. Remove from the heat and allow to cool. Add the amchoor, fresh coriander, lemon juice and garam masala. Check for seasoning.

Divide the dough into equal portions and then roll each piece into 5-cm/2-inch circles. Place a spoonful of mixture on to each and roll into a smooth ball. Flatten and roll out into a 10-cm/4-inch round disc, using a little flour if necessary, to prevent the breads from sticking.

Heat the oil in a wok, add the breads one at a time and cook over a low heat until golden brown and crisp. Drain on kitchen paper to remove any excess oil. Serve hot with Tamarind chutney.

CHANDINI KORMA

Morels in a yoghurt sauce

SERVES 4

80 g/3 oz large dried morels
2 tablespoons vegetable oil
2 tablespoons ginger and garlic paste (see page 30)
½ teaspoon ground turmeric
I teaspoon chilli powder
I teaspoon ground coriander
2 carrots, finely diced
80 g/3 oz fine beans, chopped
I potato, cooked and grated
100 g/3½ oz paneer, grated
salt, to taste
few sprigs fresh coriander, chopped
½ teaspoon garam masala

FOR THE SAUCE

I onion, chopped
60 g/2 oz cashew nuts
4 green cardamom pods
2 green chillies
3 tablespoons oil
½ teaspoon caraway seeds
2 tablespoons ginger and garlic paste (see page 30)
2 tablespoons plain yoghurt
2 tablespoons single cream
salt, to taste
I teaspoon garam masala

Wash the morels thoroughly to remove all the grit. Soak in water for I hour to rehydrate. Drain and cut off the stems, reserving the remaining parts of the morels. Blend the stems to a fine purée. Set both the morels and the purée aside.

Heat 2 tablespoons of oil in a large pan, add the ginger and garlic paste, turmeric, chilli powder, ground coriander and cook for I–2 minutes. Add the carrots and beans and cook until tender. Add the grated potato and paneer and sauté the mixture for 2 minutes. Adjust the seasoning and finish with chopped fresh coriander and garam masala. Allow to cool and then stuff the morels with this mixture. Set aside.

To make the sauce, simmer the onion, cashew nuts, cardamom pods and green chillies in 100 ml/3½ fl oz water for 10 minutes. Drain, cool and blend to a smooth paste. Set aside.

Heat the oil in a pan, add the caraway seeds and allow them to crackle then add the ginger and garlic paste and the onion and cashew nut paste. Sauté for I–2 minutes.

Whisk the yoghurt with a little water, add to the pan and mixture and stir continuously for about 8 minutes, over a medium high heat.

Add the puréed morel stems. Simmer gently, stirring occasionally, until thick. Stir in the cream and simmer for I minute.

Add the stuffed morels to the sauce, adjust the seasoning and sprinkle over the garam masala.

Khatta Meetha Kadhu

Sweet and sour pumpkin masala

SERVES 4

500 g/1 lb 2 oz pumpkin

3 tablespoons vegetable oil

3 bay leaves

½ teaspoon fenugreek seeds

2.5-cm/1-inch piece ginger, peeled and chopped

3 green chillies, chopped

½ teaspoon ground turmeric

1 teaspoon chilli powder

1½ teaspoons ground coriander

salt, to taste

1 unripe green mango, sliced

30 g/1¼ oz jaggery, grated

1 teaspoon amchoor (dried mango powder)

few sprigs fresh coriander, chopped

Cut the pumpkin into bite-sized pieces, leaving the skin on.

Heat the oil in a large pan and add the bay leaves and fenugreek seeds. Add the ginger and chillies and cook for 1–2 minutes. Add the pumpkin pieces and stir-fry for 3–4 minutes. Add the turmeric, chilli powder, ground coriander and salt. Cover and cook over a low heat for 15 minutes or until half done.

Add the green mango slices and grated jaggery. Cover and cook till soft over a low heat, stirring occasionally.

Turn off the heat and add the amchoor and chopped fresh coriander. Adjust the seasoning and serve hot.

Note This goes well with Potato curry with deep-fried bread (see page 58).

Bharwan Mircha

Pan-fried stuffed chillies

SERVES 4

4 red banana chillies (very large chillies for stuffing)

FOR THE STUFFING

3 tablespoons vegetable oil, plus extra for frying

1 teaspoon mustard seeds

2.5-cm/1-inch piece ginger, peeled and chopped

2 green chillies, chopped

few curry leaves, chopped

2 carrots, peeled and very finely diced

60 g/2 oz peas, defrosted if frozen

3 potatoes, boiled and very finely diced

1 teaspoon ground turmeric

1 teaspoon chilli powder

salt, to taste

$^1/_2$ teaspoon garam masala

juice of 1 lemon

30 g/1$^1/_4$ oz Cheddar cheese, grated

2 tablespoons Mint and coriander chutney (see page 133)

Cut the chillies in half lengthwise, deseed and set aside.

Make the stuffing. Heat 3 tablespoons oil in a pan, add the mustard seeds and allow them to crackle. Add the ginger, green chillies and curry leaves and sauté for 1 minute.

Add the carrot and green peas and cook until soft. Add the potatoes, turmeric, chilli powder and salt. Cook for 2–3 minutes. Sprinkle over the garam masala and lemon juice and check for seasoning. Turn off the heat and allow the mixture to cool.

Once cold, add the grated cheese and Mint and coriander chutney. Stuff the chillies with this mixture.

Heat a non-stick pan, add oil and cook the chillies for 1–2 minutes on each side over a low heat, turning regularly until golden. Make sure that the stuffing does not ooze out.

Mutter Makhaney

Stir-fried lotus puffs and peas

SERVES 4

oil, for deep-frying

200 g/7 oz lotus puffs

200 g/7 oz peas, defrosted if frozen

25 g/1 oz cashew nuts

15 g/½ oz melon seeds (optional)

4 green chillies

1 onion, roughly chopped

3 tablespoons oil

6 green cardamom pods

4 bay leaves

1 cinnamon stick

1 teaspoon ginger and garlic paste (see page 30)

60 g/2 oz plain yoghurt, whisked with ¼ cup water

30 g/1¼ oz khoya, grated

2 tablespoons single cream

salt, to taste

½ teaspoon garam masala

Heat the oil and deep-fry the lotus puffs until light brown. Drain on kitchen paper and set aside. Cook the peas in boiling water for 2–3 minutes. Drain and set aside.

Put the cashew nuts in a pan together with the melon seeds (if using), green chillies and onions. Add enough water to cover and simmer until the onions are soft. Drain, cool and blend to a smooth paste. Set aside.

Heat the oil in a pan and add the green cardamom pods, bay leaves and cinnamon stick. Once the spices start crackling, add the ginger and garlic paste and yoghurt and cook for 3–4 minutes. Add the onion and cashew nut paste and cook until the oil separates. Add the grated khoya and cream and cook gently for 3–5 minutes.

Add the green peas and fried lotus puffs and cook, stirring for about 4–5 minutes. Adjust the seasoning and finish with garam masala.

LUCKNOW

LUCKNOW IS A CITY that has been in my consciousness for many years. When I used to work at Radio Scotland I discovered that Lucknow was India's raciest city, in terms of bizarre sexual practices. Apparently there are more orgies in Lucknow that anywhere else on the sub-continent. The mind boggles. Clearly a city that enjoys such hedonistic sensuality will no doubt have much to offer in terms of food. Where there is the carnal there is invariably the cuisinal...

Lucknow is steeped and soaked in history; glorious history. The Mughal grasp stretched out East and the Awadh area and Lucknow were at its heart. With the Mughals came beautifully manicured gardens, breath-taking architecture, romantic poetry and amazing food, inspired by their Persian antecedents. The Nawabs or rulers of Lucknow were renowned for their culture and such was the prominence of Lucknow it became known as The Constantinople of India. The Awadh region itself is one of the most fecund in India, benefitting from the naturally irrigated plain between the River Ganges and the River Yamuna. No doubt the agriculture that was spawned from such fertility required transportation links and hence the presence of the GT Road.

Being of Punjabi stock myself, from close to the border with Pakistan, I have some experience of the delights of Mughal-influenced food. If ever a culture was reflected in food, look no further than the Mughals. There is a definite link between their approach to cooking, their approach to textile, their approach to architecture, their very lifestyle. The majesty of their buildings, their dazzling costumes, the richness of their culture... all can be found in their amazingly august, bejewelled, rich food.

HAZRATH GUNJ AND THE QUEST FOR BIRYANI

It took some time to find the biryani place. I couldn't think of any better way to dive into the Mughal way of eating than with biryani. There is no greater metaphor for the Mughal than their deliciously indulgent rich dishes. For those that have only ever experienced biryani late on a Friday night, in the wake of a skinful of over-carbonated beer in a restaurant with the word 'Raj', 'Days' and 'of' in the title, prepare for your monochrome world to collide with the technicolour of historical reality.

Off a roundabout in the old town, past the YMCA is a small parade of shop fronts. Between a fish tank shop and Pakeeza Juice Corner nestles a grotty-looking cafe. Now I have, in my time, managed to divorce the look of a place with the food on offer; I live in the East End of London, after all. Pristine

restaurants have served some of the most awful food I have eaten; formica-topped cafe tables have become yet another road to my Damascus of food delight. This place looks terrible. Unapologetically terrible. But the food is highly recommended. A few tired-looking marble steps offer some sort of welcome. The food certainly smells good but is too high to view from street level. I brace myself and my stomach and climb up the marble, wondering if it will be some stairway to biryani heaven...

I had come for the biryani but as I step up my magpie eyes spy a large tava with scores of delicious shammi kebabs grilling away gorgeously. Biryani can wait.

The shammi kebab is a blend of mutton and lentils, flavoured with onion and a handful of spices. There is a clean simplicity to the flavours.

As I tucked into my delicious kebab I realised that this wasn't the legendary biryani place I needed to visit. No. Mid-mouthful I tried to ascertain my exact location. There was a great deal of confusion, even amongst the locals, as to where I was and where I desired to be, so no great surprise I wasn't clear myself. The place I wanted was somewhere around the corner. I looked out the front of the shop... all I could see were corners... corners, corners everywhere but no mutton biryani in sight.

If ever in doubt about where you are or where you need to be, ask not at some fancy hotel; bother not a taxi driver; the fonts of all knowledge are the rickshaw wallahs. Admittedly I had to interrogate half a dozen or so of the cycle carriers but eventually I had nothing but mutton biryani in my cross-hairs.

Naushijaan Lazzate-e-Lucknow offers any manner of biryani. Dumpuqt, Deghi, Hyderbadi. All different, all delicious. I've opted for the Dumpuqt Mutton and a little side of mutton curry. The dumpuqt comes in a small earthenware dish that has had its lid sealed on with dough. This traps the steam and allows the dish to cook without losing any flavour. And what flavour! The meat has cooked in its captive juices and there is an elegant simplicity about the combination of rice and mutton. A little pot of natural yoghurt is a heavenly companion. Paradise.

It seems fitting that in such a regal city I attempt to make contact with one of the members of royalty.

Lo and behold, Rajkumar Amir Naqi Khan has invited me to take tea. Tea — with a Nawab. The Nawab of Mahmudabad. And I'm wearing Adidas tracksuit trousers.

His forebears came from Multan (in modern day Pakistan) in the twelfth century. The family ruled and governed the area ever since and the palace I am sitting in was built by his grandfather. Luckily for me, the Nawab is a food lover and takes some time to explain the history of the development of food in and around Lucknow. The Turks had a presence in Lucknow as far back as the twelfth century and with them brought the idea of korma and a rice dish they called pilaf, hence the urdu word 'pilau' for certain rice dishes. A couple of hundred years later the Iranian influence was felt and with it more of the Mughlai dishes entered the everyday food vocabulary of Awadh.

In the twelfth century the Turks brought korma and pilaff. Biryani was brought from Iraq. In fourteenth-century Awadh Iranian influences were strong because Nawab was Iranian. Mughlai influences were also strong. Such was the prosperity of the times, and the drama of the food that the Nawab tells me of a famous and now seldom prepared diah, Kundun Kalia. This is a type of meat korma finished with gold leaf... a hugely expensive dish that was very much for high days and holidays. I imagine how it must have tasted as I bite on a digestive biscuit and sip my tea. I point out that I have found very few vegetable dishes in Lucknow. He laughs a regal, well-educated laugh. He tells me that the Mughals had no interest in vegetables; they were very much an afterthought. Mughlai cooking is all about the meat. Like I said, I must have Mughal blood in me somewhere...

79

OLD TOWN

After a mandatory post-prandial nap the evening insisted a visit to the Old Town. Colonnaded buildings offered shabby chic at its shabbiest and chicest. One can only wonder about how palatial a city this must have been when the Mughals were in full swing. There are food stalls everywhere. Juice men hawk their wares; shammi kebabs and parathas aplenty, sweet stands bejewelled with pink, yellow, orange sweetmeats. Walking into the old town complex takes you back hundreds of years; the food will have changed very little since then. A four-storey building, ramshackle and one-off, reaches upwards either side of the narrow lanes and byways. It feels as if all of human life resides here or there; everything is so immediate. People, cycles, scooters, food and cows; all within constant and continual touching distance. I meander and dodge and dance my way along this vein of vibrancy, this aorta of activity to the heart of the Old Town and the promise of food.

I enter a place famous for a special type of kebab. I have only ever heard of Galavati Kebab. And this anonymous shack serves only Galavati Kebab. Nothing else. So it's Galavati Kebab or nothing. And nothing is never an option.

Like so many of the best places to eat on the GT Road, judgeth not the shop by its front. Here, half a dozen or so men sit around various cooking areas. The entire space is dominated by a massive tava, the largest I have seen yet. A large bowl of unappetising meat mixture is rolled and manipulated into small balls that are then flattened and fried. Meanwhile fresh buttered parathas are made... that is the recipe for success.

The kebab itself looks innocuous enough; but it packs some punch. The spices sing, in the choral tradition. Next to us a young family of five rip into their kebabs. They come every fortnight. Why? They love the tradition and the price; a fraction of what inferior versions cost in the gleaming new shopping malls that are reinventing the landscape of urban India.

I need tea after the sensual attack of the Galavati Kebab. I wander in search of a change of surrounding and a cup of hot, sweet Indian tea. I discover a sight I have never before witnessed in all my visits to India. Blanketed men huddle round a tea seller sipping a bright pink liquid from glasses, the steam rising off the top in the cold evening air. This is Kashmiri tea and it is some distance from home. This is yet another reflection of the cosmopolitan nature of Lucknow; it has sucked souls from all over India into its hinterland. The tea is sweet and milky and comforting. A second cup imbibed, I feel satiated. For now.

Lauki ke Koftey

Bottle gourd dumplings in a yoghurt sauce

MAKES 4

FOR THE DUMPLINGS

1 kg/2 lb 4 oz lauki (bottle gourd)

2.5-cm/1-inch piece ginger, peeled and chopped

4 green chillies, chopped

100 g/3½ oz chickpea flour

½ teaspoon ground cumin

1 teaspoon carom seeds

1 teaspoon ground coriander

1 teaspoon chilli powder

¼ teaspoon ground turmeric

½ teaspoon garam masala

few sprigs fresh coriander, chopped

salt, to taste

vegetable oil, for frying

FOR THE SAUCE

3 onions, roughly chopped

3 green chillies, deseeded

2 tomatoes

50 g/2 oz plain yoghurt

3 tablespoons vegetable oil

4 bay leaves

1 teaspoon ginger and garlic paste (see page 30)

¼ teaspoon ground turmeric

1 teaspoon chilli powder

1 teaspoon ground coriander

salt, to taste

½ teaspoon ground fenugreek

½ teaspoon garam masala

few sprigs fresh coriander, chopped

First make the dumplings. Wash and grate the lauki, squeezing out the excess water and then place in a large bowl.

Add the ginger, chopped chillies, chickpea flour, cumin, carom seeds, ground coriander, chilli powder, turmeric, garam masala, chopped fresh coriander and salt to the lauki and mix well. Shape into small round dumplings.

Heat enough oil for deep-frying in a deep frying pan or wok to 180°C/350°F, or until a cube of bread browns in 30 seconds. Fry the dumplings until crisp and golden brown. Drain on kitchen paper and set aside.

For the sauce, blend the onions and green chillies in a food processor to a fine paste. Blend the tomatoes to a smooth purée. Whisk the yoghurt with ½ cup of water and set aside. Heat the oil in a pan and add the bay leaves. Allow to infuse. Add the onion and green chilli paste and cook until golden brown. Add the ginger and garlic paste, turmeric, chilli powder, ground coriander and salt and sauté for 2 minutes. Add the puréed tomatoes, cover and cook for 4–5 minutes. Add the yoghurt and cook until the oil separates. Add 2 cups of water and bring to the boil, then stir in the fenugreek.

Add the fried dumplings and gently simmer in the sauce for 10–15 minutes or until the koftas are soft. Finish with garam masala and chopped fresh coriander.

PITHIWALI TIKKI

Potato cakes with tangy lentil filling

SERVES 4

4 large potatoes

salt, to taste

¼ teaspoon ground nutmeg

2 tablespoons roasted chana powder

I tablespoon cornflour

FOR THE FILLING

150 g/5½ oz urad dal (white lentils)

50 ml/2 fl oz vegetable oil

½ teaspoon cumin seeds

2.5-cm/I-inch piece ginger, peeled and chopped

3 green chillies, chopped

pinch of asafoetida

I teaspoon chilli powder

I teaspoon ground coriander

¼ teaspoon ground turmeric

salt, to taste

I tablespoon amchoor (dried mango powder)

few sprigs fresh coriander, chopped

juice of I lemon

I teaspoon garam masala

Wash the potatoes, boil and cool. (Allow them to cool overnight or for at least 2–3 hours to let the starch settle). Peel and grate potatoes. Add salt, nutmeg, roasted chana powder and cornflour and mix. Use your hands to mix thoroughly, making sure all the ingredients are combined. Divide into 8–10 portions and set aside.

For the filling, wash the lentils and soak for at least 2 hours in cold water. Drain and set aside.

Heat I tablespoon oil in a pan, add the cumin seeds and allow them to crackle. Add the ginger, green chilli and asafoetida and stir for I minute. Add the soaked lentils, chilli powder, ground coriander, turmeric and salt. Cook, stirring, for 4–5 minutes. Allow the stuffing to cool, then add the amchoor, chopped fresh coriander and lemon juice. Check for seasoning and sprinkle over the garam masala.

Flatten the potato portions into small round discs and press your thumb into the centre of each one. Place a spoonful of stuffing in the centre and seal the edges, making sure that the stuffing does not come out. Press the stuffed potato cakes gently and flatten them again to a round shape.

Heat the remaining oil in a non-stick pan and shallow-fry the cakes over a low heat until crisp and golden brown.

Serve hot with Tamarind chutney (see page 132) and Mint and coriander chutney (see page 133).

MURGH MUSALLAM

Whole braised baby chicken

SERVES 4

2 poussins

2 tablespoons ginger and garlic paste (see page 30)

1 teaspoon chilli powder

4 tablespoons vegetable oil

salt, to taste

juice of 1 lemon

FOR THE STUFFING

2 eggs

100 g/3½ oz chicken mince

2.5-cm/1-inch piece ginger, peeled and finely grated

3 green chillies, chopped

few sprigs coriander, chopped

15 g/¼ oz golden raisins

10 g/¼ oz pistachios

10 g/¼ oz cashew nuts, chopped

1 teaspoon chilli powder

1 teaspoon garam masala

large pinch saffron strands

few sprigs mint, chopped

¼ teaspoon ground cardamom

¼ teaspoon ground mace

salt, to taste

FOR THE SAUCE

4 tablespoons vegetable oil

2 onions, sliced

2 tablespoons yoghurt

40 g/1½ oz skinned almonds

3 tomatoes

3 bay leaves

4 green cardamom pods

1 cinnamon stick

1 tablespoon ginger and garlic paste (see page 30)

2 teaspoons chilli powder

few drops kewra water

few sprigs coriander, chopped

few sprigs mint, chopped

pinch saffron strands

½ teaspoon ground cardamom

¼ teaspoon ground mace

salt, to taste

2.5-cm/1-inch piece ginger, peeled and cut into julienne

chopped fresh coriander, to garnish

Clean and wash the poussins. Drain and pat dry. Put the ginger and garlic paste, chilli powder, 2 tablespoons of oil, salt and lemon juice in a large bowl and mix well.

Rub this mixture over the poussins and leave to marinate for at least 2 hours. Cover and refrigerate.

Now make the stuffing. Hard boil the eggs for 8–10 minutes. Cool, peel and keep aside. In a large mixing bowl, add chicken mince, ginger, green chilli, fresh coriander, raisins, pistachios, broken cashew nuts, chilli powder, garam masala, saffron, mint, cardamom, mace and salt. Mix well.

Divide the mixture into two. Wrap each boiled egg with chicken mince and stuff inside the poussins. Truss the poussins with a trussing needle. Make sure poussins are well sealed and the stuffing is held in place.

Heat 2 tablespoons oil in a wok or large frying pan. Sear the poussins until golden brown on all sides, then remove from the pan and drain on kitchen paper.

To make the sauce heat 2 tablespoons of oil in pan, add the sliced onion and fry until golden brown. Drain on absorbent kitchen paper and then place in a food processor with the yoghurt. Blend until you have a smooth paste and set aside.

Place the almonds in a small pan of water, bring to the boil and simmer for about 15 minutes. Drain, cool and then transfer to a food processor and blend to a smooth paste. Blend the tomatoes to a fine purée in a food processor and set aside.

Heat 2 tablespoons oil in a large lidded heavy-based pan; once the oil is hot add bay leaves, green cardamom pods and cinnamon sticks and allow to infuse.

Add the ginger and garlic paste and sauté for 2 minutes. Add the fried onion yoghurt paste, cover and cook on medium heat for 6–7 minutes. Add chilli powder and salt. Mix well.

Add the tomato purée and cook until the oil separates. Add the almond paste and 3 cups of water. Cover and cook on a low heat for 10 minutes.

Preheat the oven to 200°C/400°F/gas 6. Add the poussins to the pan and gently simmer for 5–6 minutes. Cover the pan with a tightly fitting lid and place in the oven. Cook for 20–25 minutes until poussins are tender.

Remove the poussins, discard the string and arrange on a clean platter.

Reduce the sauce till thick, add kewra water, fresh coriander, mint, saffron, cardamom and mace. Cook for a further 1–2 minutes.

Adjust the seasoning and coat the poussins with the sauce. Garnish with chopped coriander and ginger julienne.

Dum ka Batera

Stuffed quail

SERVES 4

8 quail
1 tablespoon ginger and garlic paste
(see page 30)
½ teaspoon chilli powder
juice of 1 lemon
salt, to taste
vegetable oil, for frying

FOR THE STUFFING

200 g/7 oz chicken mince
2.5-cm/1-inch piece ginger, chopped
2 green chillies, chopped
few sprigs fresh coriander, chopped
¼ teaspoon ground mace
¼ teaspoon ground cardamom
½ teaspoon garam masala
pinch of saffron strands
20 g/1 oz Cheddar cheese, grated
½ teaspoon chilli powder
salt, to taste
8 quail's eggs, hard-boiled and peeled

FOR THE SAUCE

3 tomatoes
50 g/2 oz cashew nuts
2 onions, sliced
50 g/2 oz plain yoghurt
3 green chillies
4 green cardamom pods
4 bay leaves
2 cinnamon sticks
1 teaspoon chilli powder
salt, to taste
1 teaspoon garam masala
few sprigs fresh coriander, chopped

Wash the quail inside and out. Drain and pat dry. Put the ginger and garlic paste, chilli powder, lemon juice and salt in a bowl and mix well. Rub this mixture over the quail and set aside to marinate for 20 minutes.

Make the stuffing. Put the chicken mince, ginger, green chillies, fresh coriander, mace, cardamom, garam masala, saffron, grated cheese, chilli powder and salt into a large bowl. Mix well. Stuff each quail with the chicken mixture then push a boiled quail's egg into the centre of the mince. Secure the opening of each quail with kitchen string. Heat 1 tablespoon of oil in a non-stick pan and brown the stuffed quail all over. Set aside.

Make the sauce. Blend the tomatoes to a smooth purée in a food processor. Set aside.

Fry the cashew nuts in 3 tablespoons of oil then drain on kitchen paper and set aside. Add the sliced onions to the same oil and fry until golden brown then drain on kitchen paper. Place the fried cashew nuts, fried onions, yoghurt and green chillies in a food processor and blend to a smooth paste.

Heat 2 tablespoons oil in a large casserole and add the green cardamom pods, bay leaves and cinnamon sticks. When they start to crackle, add the cashew nut and onion paste and cook for 7–8 minutes. Add chilli and salt. Add the puréed tomatoes and cook for 5 minutes or until the oil separates.

Add the quail to the sauce, cover and cook over a low heat until tender. Alternatively place the pot, in an oven preheated to 180°C/350°F/gas 5 and cook for 30–40 minutes. Sprinkle over garam masala and chopped fresh coriander to serve.

Galavat ke Kebab

Smoked lamb patties

SERVES 4

500 g/1 lb 2 oz boneless lamb from the leg, diced

100 g/4 oz lamb fat (ask your butcher)

1 onion, sliced

50 g/2 oz cashew nuts

4 green chillies

1 tablespoon ginger and garlic paste (see page 30)

2 tablespoons papaya paste (see page 219)

$^1/_2$ teaspoon garam masala

1 teaspoon chilli powder

$^1/_4$ teaspoon ground mace

$^1/_4$ teaspoon ground cardamom

pinch of ground nutmeg

60 g/2$^1/_2$ oz roasted chana powder (see page 219)

6 tablespoons ghee

large pinch saffron strands

few sprigs fresh mint, chopped

salt, to taste

chopped tomato, red onion and cucumber, to serve

Combine the diced lamb and lamb fat. Blend in a food processor until finely minced.

Fry the sliced onion, cashew nuts and green chillies until golden brown, drain on kitchen paper and blend to a fine paste in a food processor, adding water if required. Set aside.

Put the minced lamb, ginger and garlic paste, papaya paste, and the onion, cashew nut and green chilli paste in a large bowl. Mix well. Add the garam masala, chilli powder, mace, cardamom, nutmeg and roasted chana powder. Add 4 tablespoons ghee, the saffron, chopped fresh mint and salt. Mix until thoroughly combined.

For an authentic smoky flavour you can now smoke the lamb. Tip the lamb mixture into a large roasting tray with deep sides. Place a hot piece of charcoal in a small metal bowl and place it in the middle of the roasting tray. Pour a teaspoon of ghee onto the charcoal and then cover the roasting tray with a lid or some aluminium foil, trapping the smoke inside. Leave to stand for 5 minutes. Discard the charcoal and mix well. Divide the mixture into balls and then press them gently to make flat patties.

Heat the remaining ghee in a non-stick pan and fry the patties one at a time, for about 1 minute on each side. Turn and cook over a medium heat until golden brown on both sides. Serve with chopped tomato, red onion and cucumber.

SHAMMI KEBAB

Lamb patties

SERVES 4

800 g/1 lb 12 oz boneless
lamb, diced

80 g/3 oz chana dal (yellow
split peas)

4 green cardamom pods

4 black cardamom pods

1 teaspoon fennel seeds

2 blades mace

1 cinnamon stick

4 bay leaves

8 black peppercorns

2.5-cm/1-inch piece ginger,
peeled and roughly chopped

8 cloves garlic

3 green chillies

1 tablespoon chilli powder

1 teaspoon ground turmeric

salt, to taste

few sprigs fresh mint, chopped

1 onion, chopped

1 egg

1 tablespoon cornflour

1 teaspoon garam masala

3 tablespoons double cream

1 tablespoon ghee

vegetable oil, for deep-frying

Mint and coriander chutney
(see page 133) and Tamarind
chutney (see page 132), to
serve

Put the lamb, lentils, green and black cardamom pods, fennel seeds, mace, cinnamon stick, bay leaves, black peppercorns, ginger, garlic, green chillies, chilli powder, turmeric and salt in a large pan. Add enough water to cover the meat and bring to the boil. Reduce the heat to medium and cook until the lamb is tender and the water has evaporated. Tip the mixture into a shallow dish and allow to cool. Discard the whole spices and then transfer the meat to a mincer and mince it twice.

Put the minced lamb in a large mixing bowl; add the fresh mint, chopped onion, egg, cornflour, garam masala, double cream and ghee. Mix well. Divide the mixture into balls and roll into smooth dumplings. Press the dumplings to flatten.

Heat the oil in a wok, add the patties, a few at a time, and fry over a medium heat until crisp and golden brown. Drain on kitchen paper and serve hot with Mint and coriander chutney and Tamarind chutney.

Dum Biryani

Lamb and basmati rice

SERVES 4

3 tablespoons vegetable oil

4 onions, sliced

100 g/4 oz ghee

4 bay leaves

2 blades mace

5–6 green cardamom pods

2 cinnamon sticks

4 green chillies

700 g/1½ lbs boneless lamb,
cut into 2-cm/¾-inch pieces

2 tablespoons ginger and garlic
paste (see page 30)

1 teaspoon chilli powder

salt, to taste

125 g/4 oz plain yoghurt

1 tablespoon garam masala

2.5-cm/1-inch piece ginger,
peeled and cut into julienne

80 ml/3 fl oz single cream

¼ teaspoon ground cardamom

¼ teaspoon ground mace

½ teaspoon kewra water

few sprigs fresh mint, chopped

few saffron strands

FOR THE RICE

500 g/1 lb 2 oz basmati rice

3 tablespoons oil

salt, to taste

4 green cardamom pods

2 blades mace

First make the rice. Wash and soak the rice for 30 minutes. Bring water to the boil in a large pan. Add the oil, salt, green cardamom pods and mace blades. Allow to infuse, add the soaked rice and cook until half done, about 7–8 minutes. Drain and set aside.

Heat the oil in a wok, add half the sliced onions and fry until golden brown then drain on kitchen paper and set aside.

Heat the ghee in a large lidded casserole and add the bay leaves, mace blades, ground green cardamom pods and cinnamon. Allow to infuse.

Add the green chillies and remaining sliced onions and cook until golden brown. Add the lamb and cook over a medium heat until browned. Add the ginger and garlic paste and cook for 2 minutes. Add the chilli powder and salt. Mix well.

Whisk the yoghurt with 1 cup of water and add it to the lamb. Cook for 5 minutes, stirring continuously. Add enough water to cover and cook over a medium heat until tender. Add half of the garam masala, the ginger strips, cream, ground cardamom, mace and kewra water. Cook, stirring for 2–3 minutes. Preheat the oven to 180°C/350°F/gas 5.

Layer the cooked rice on top of the lamb, sprinkle with the reserved browned onions, mint and saffron. Cover tightly and cook in the oven for 30–40 minutes. Do not remove the lid until you are ready to serve.

Note Traditionally, the pot would be sealed with a strip of dough pressed around the lid to trap the moisture inside and then cooked over a charcoal fire. If you don't have any dough to hand, use foil or greaseproof paper tied with string.

91

Dabi Arbi ka Salan

Lamb and Indian yam curry

SERVES 4

500 g/1 lb 2 oz colocasia
(Indian yam)

3 tablespoons vegetable oil

3 onions, sliced

1 kg/2 lb 4 oz boneless lamb

1 tablespoon ginger and garlic
paste (see page 30)

1 teaspoon ground turmeric

2 teaspoons chilli powder

salt, to taste

3 cloves

6 green cardamom pods

2 cinnamon sticks

2 teaspoons ground coriander

1/2 teaspoon black peppercorns,
crushed

1/4 teaspoon ground cardamom

1/4 teaspoon ground mace

2 tablespoons plain yoghurt

FOR THE SALAN MASALA

2 tablespoons coriander seeds

1/4 teaspoon ground sandalwood

2 bay leaves

1/2 teaspoon dried rose petals

2 black cardamom pods

1/2 cinnamon stick

1/2 teaspoon fennel seeds

2 blades mace

1/4 teaspoon ground ginger

Place all the ingredients for the salan masala in a blender. Blend to a fine powder. Set aside.

Cook the yam in a large pan of boiling water for 15–20 minutes. Drain. When cool enough to handle, peel and press flat. Set aside.

Heat the oil in a pan, add half the sliced onions and cook until golden brown. Cut the lamb into 2-cm/3/4-inch pieces and add to the pan. Cook over a high heat for 3–4 minutes until browned.

Add the ginger and garlic paste and cook for 2 minutes. Add the turmeric, chilli powder, salt, cloves, green cardamom pods and cinnamon sticks. Mix well.

Add the remaining sliced onions and sauté for 2–3 minutes. Add 2 cups of water, cover and cook over a low heat for about 15 minutes.

Add the coriander, crushed black peppercorns, cardamom, mace and yoghurt. Mix well, cover and cook for a further 10 minutes, until the meat is tender.

Shallow-fry the pressed yam for about 5 minutes and then add to the lamb. Adjust the seasoning and sprinkle over 1 tablespoon of the salan masala and mix. Serve hot.

Guchhi Pulao

Morels cooked with basmati rice

SERVES 4

1 kg/2 lb 4 oz basmati rice

100 g/3½ oz dried morels

3 tablespoons vegetable oil

4 green cardamom pods

2 black cardamom pods

1 cinnamon stick

3 bay leaves

2 blades mace

1 teaspoon cumin seeds

40 g/1½ oz butter

100 ml/3½ fl oz single cream

salt, to taste

Put the rice in a colander, rinse under cold running water and then leave to soak in cold water for at least 1 hour. Soak the dried morels in a bowl of warm water for 20 minutes. Drain and rinse well in cold water to remove any grit. Cut into quarters.

Heat the oil in a pan and add the green and black cardamom pods, cinnamon, bay leaves and mace blades. Allow to infuse.

Add the cumin seeds and allow them to crackle, add the morels and fry for a few seconds. Pour in 1 litre/2 pints water and bring to the boil. Add the butter, cream and salt and bring to the boil once more.

Add the soaked rice and cook over a low heat for about 3–4 minutes, or until the water is absorbed.

Cover the rice with a clean damp cloth. Cover the pan with a tight lid.

Heat a griddle pan over a low heat and place the covered pan on it. Cook for 25–30 minutes. Alternatively cook in a pre-heated oven at 180°C/350°F/gas 5 for 10–12 minutes or until done. Mix gently and serve hot.

Palak Anjeer ki Tikki

Pan-fried spinach cakes stuffed with figs

SERVES 4

400 g/14 oz fresh spinach

100 g/3½ oz chana dal (yellow split peas)

1 tablespoon cornflour

2.5-cm/1-inch piece ginger, peeled and chopped

2 green chillies, chopped

1 teaspoon ground cumin

1 teaspoon garam masala

¼ teaspoon ground fenugreek

salt, to taste

2 tablespoons vegetable oil

Tamarind chutney (see page 132), to serve

FOR THE FILLING

8 dried figs, chopped

2 tablespoons mascarpone

2 tablespoons hung yoghurt yoghurt (see page 218)

½ teaspoon ground cumin

2.5-cm/1-inch piece ginger, peeled and chopped

1 green chilli, chopped

salt, to taste

Cut and discard the spinach stalks. Wash the leaves and then cook in the water clinging to the leaves until just wilted. Drain, refresh in cold water and set aside.

Boil the chana dal for 10 minutes, until cooked, but not too soft. Drain and cool and then place in a food processor or blender with the spinach leaves. Process briefly until you have a coarse paste. Transfer to a large bowl and add the cornflour, ginger, chillies, cumin, garam masala, fenugreek and salt. Mix well. Divide the mixture into equal-sized balls and set aside.

Make the filling. Put the dried figs, mascarpone, yoghurt, cumin, ginger, green chilli and salt in a bowl and mix well.

Flatten each spinach ball into a round patty about 1 cm/½ inch thick and place ½ teaspoon of fig yoghurt stuffing in the centre. Fold the edges together, making sure that the stuffing does not come out. Flatten the filled patties again.

Heat the oil in a non-stick pan and add the stuffed spinach patties one at a time. Fry over a low heat on both sides until crisp and golden brown. Serve hot with Tamarind chutney.

Aam ki Laung

Green mango chutney

SERVES 4

700 g/1 lb 9 oz unripe green mangoes

75 ml/2½ fl oz mustard oil

1 teaspoon panch phoran (see page 210)

3 green chillies, slit lengthways

1 teaspoon chilli powder

1 teaspoon ground coriander

½ teaspoon ground turmeric

salt, to taste

150 g/5½ oz jaggery, grated

Wash, wipe and slice the mangoes, keeping the skin on. Set aside.

Heat the oil in pan, add the panch phoran and allow it to crackle. Once crackled add the green chillies and sliced mangoes. Cook for 10–12 minutes over a low heat until the mangoes turn soft.

Add the chilli powder, coriander, turmeric and salt. Mix well. Sprinkle over 4 tablespoons of water and the jaggery. Cook until the jaggery melts and thickens.

Turn off the heat. Cool and store in an airtight container.

Papeetey ka Murabba

Chunky green papaya chutney

SERVES 4

2 tablespoons vegetable oil

1 teaspoon onion seeds

1 teaspoon fennel seeds

4 red chillies

500 g/1 lb 2 oz green papaya, peeled and sliced

300 g/11 oz caster sugar

150 ml/5½ fl oz water

80 ml/3 fl oz white vinegar

salt, to taste

Heat the oil in a pan and add the onion seeds, fennel seeds and whole red chillies. Allow the seeds to crackle and then add the sliced papaya and cook for 5–7 minutes. Add the sugar and water to the pan and bring to the boil.

Add the white vinegar and simmer the mixture for 10 minutes or until the syrup thickens and coats the papaya. Add salt to taste. Turn off the heat, cool and store in an airtight container.

Aamley ki Chutney

Sweet gooseberry chutney

SERVES 4

1 kg/2 lb 4 oz gooseberries

1 tablespoon bicarbonate of soda

850 g/1 lb 14 oz caster sugar

40 ml/2 fl oz vegetable oil

6 black cardamom pods

1 tablespoon panch phoran (see page 210)

2.5-cm/1-inch piece ginger, peeled and chopped

3 green chillies, chopped

salt, to taste

pinch of saffron strands

2 tablespoons white vinegar

Soak the gooseberries overnight in enough water to cover, mixed with the bicarbonate of soda. The following day, discard the water and rinse and drain the gooseberries. Place the gooseberries in a large pan of water and bring to the boil. Reduce the heat and simmer for about 10 minutes, until the gooseberries are soft and tender. Drain and set aside. Deseed when cool.

Put the sugar in a heavy-based saucepan and add 500 ml/18 fl oz of water. Bring to the boil and cook for 10–12 minutes. Add the gooseberries and continue to cook over a low heat.

Meanwhile, heat the oil in a pan, add the black cardamom pods and allow to infuse. Add the panch phoran and allow it to crackle. Once crackled add the chopped ginger and green chillies and cook for 2–3 minutes.

Add the ginger chilli mixture to the gooseberries and cook for 10–15 minutes or until thickened. Adjust the seasoning, add the saffron and vinegar and cook for 5 minutes before turning off the heat. Cool and store in an airtight container.

PHIRNEE

Saffron rice pudding

SERVES 4

150 g/5½ oz short-grain rice

2 litres/3½ pints full-cream milk

100 g/3½ oz caster sugar

½ teaspoon ground green cardamom

few saffron strands

few pistachio slivers, to decorate

gold leaf, to decorate

Rinse the rice in a colander and soak for 1 one hour. Drain again and then transfer to a food processor or blender. Process roughly until you have a coarse paste (make sure the paste is not too fine).

Bring the milk to the boil in a heavy-based saucepan then add the rice paste and cook until thickened and the rice is cooked. This should take about 10–12 minutes. Add the sugar and cook until it dissolves and then stir in the cardamom and saffron strands.

Pour the mixture into a serving bowl or several small dishes and place in the refrigerator for at least 2 hours. Serve cold, decorated with pistachio slivers and edible gold leaf.

ALIGARGH

AN EARLY MORNING START — 7AM. The fog over Lucknow is about to be burnt off by the sun. I'm heading east out of the city on the Grand Trunk Road. This is a simple two-lane affair, a broken white line down the middle, no pavement to the left. Instead the road melts treacherously into everyday life; and everyday life occasionally darts treacherously into the road. Shops, cafes, houses, fields, a continually changing landscape to the left. And to the right? GT traffic heading Calcutta-ward.

I have eight hours in the car to look forward to. In a couple of hours we'll stop in Carnpure for breakfast; breakfast by the GT road. Then another four hours onto Agawah for lunch, hopefully. All going to plan we'd hit Aligarh by 5pm. It has to be noted that there are no individual plans on the GT road. In a country governed by religion and Fate it seems belief extends no further than the end of the bonnet. But maybe that is just my Fate?

The land either side is beautifully verdant, mistily green with the golden glow of a rising sun. Lucknow and its palaces and gardens seem a world away. From the complex cris-crossing of life in the Old Town the straight lines of the GT Road are a welcome change. Sleep beckons in the softest, most alluring of tones. I soften, I'm allured...

Three hours later I awake with a hunger that can mean only one thing: breakfast. There is one, single universal food that can be consumed at any and every point along the entire length of GT road; it's aloo ka paratha. Unleavened bread stuffed with spiced potato and shallow fried; this is only a literal translation, a translation denuded of the poetry, the romance, the glory of aloo ka paratha. I have grown up with it, coveted it, tried to make it, dreamt of it and ultimately felt it on my waistline. Aloo ka paratha has been my friend, my downfall, my first, my last, my everything. There are no words realistically robust or sufficiently superlative enough to convey the sense of how the soul is sated with such food. Simply served with 'empty' dhai (plain yoghurt) and pickles and a more than generous knob of butter, it's the quintessential Indian breakfast of champions.

There's a dhaba called Sikandera (where the new and old GT Roads meet) where aloo ka paratha is served with a simple potato and pea curry. I eschew the peas and the potatoes; eating them would feel like an infidelity. This moment is all about aloo ka paratha and me. We consummate our relationship for the thousandth time. Bliss. Carbohydrate rush. Then Slump. Are you getting some sort of idea about how I feel about aloo ka paratha?

Half an hour north of Agra and two hours from Aligarh and it's time for a cup of tea — sweet, milky and hot — at a proper roadside dhaba. As I walk up the steps I see tarka being freshly added to dal, a sign of immediate readiness: there will be no better moment to consume this bowl of lentils. Tea has become an unscheduled lunch. Hunger has been a happy stranger since I started my journey; duty is my watchword. I HAVE to eat this dal, for myriad reasons, but most compelling of them because you, dear reader, cannot.

I am greeted and waited upon by a small but perfectly formed midget. He goes about his every task in miniature, age apparent in his face if not in his stature. The dal is delicious. The rotis are hot and fresh from the tandoor. And the tea, the best yet on the GT road. The midget watches my every small move. My eyes convey my happiness. And he smiles his.

A foggy night in Aligarh. This is old GT Road territory, a ghost town that once was vibrant with the east/west, west/east traffic down the original GT Road. We are cutting through the town in search of more Mughal masterpieces; what those guys do with meat is close to unholy and so very delicious. We arrive at a concrete shop in splendid isolation.

This is a nameless place that needs no name. Everyone knows that behind the concrete is the finest Nihari and Paya for miles around. Sat four-square on the main road, the rickety door opens out immediately onto the frenetic road… men gather outside, spilling randomly into the thoroughfare. Interesting to note, but I can't recall seeing a single woman at any of the roadside dhabas I've visited. Time for me to man up. Again.

Unusually this chef, Nirala, combines two famous Mughal/Muslim dishes in one. Paya and Nihari. I cannot begin to tell you how unusual this is and this combination is unique to this place, this chef. He is the fourth man in his familial line to cook. His great grandfather cooked for the Rajas. His grandfather cooked for Rajas. His father cooked for Rajas. Tonight I feel like a Raja.

The economic reality is that modern day Rajas can't afford to keep a private cook so Nirala threw himself at the mercy of the market. He spends six or seven hours a day cooking; his food sells in less than two. Even the most basic grasp of supply-and-demand economics makes you realise how damn popular his food is.

There are in total three dishes on offer. Paya, buffalo trotters; nihari, a slow-cooked buffalo curry; and buffalo korma. The trotters are gelatinous and the sauce around similarly so. The nihari is highly spiced and delicious. The korma, a sauce that mixes the paya and nihari together: this couldn't be further from the fruity, creamy kormas you may know. This has no cream, no fruit. Just big flavour. Each dish has a unique taste individually. When combined, well… I'm lost for words…

On the road to Delhi we have been searching for barule, a deep-fried potato street snack, only found in and around this area. They are baby potatoes, lightly battered in a chick pea and pea flour, marinaded, sautéed and then deep-fried. They are served with salt, coriander, lime, red chilli, chat masala, tamarind and sour mango paste: a veritable tingle on the tastebuds. Barule is seasonal, only available when new potatoes emerge, around December/January. We slow down through every small town and village, scouring the hand-carts for signs of these oval delights. It seems almost every other street snack is on offer with the exception of barule. Having given up hope, hope comes and finds us. A lone street vendor with a decrepit cart sells barule. His indifference seems to suggest his ignorance at how rare a commodity he hawks. But thankfully he does hawk. And I eat. Deliciousness, defined by its simplicity.

BULANDSHAHR

A few hours down the GT, ever closer to Delhi and the Punjab, I stop for tea. And the mandatory snack. Choley bhaturey (chickpea curry with deep-fried bread) is a roadside special. The previously deep-fried baturey is subsequently tava-fried with lashings of butter. The smell of charcoal fills the nostrils. It's a constant roadside smell in India. (In my father's city, Ferozepur, they sell shali; whole corn cobs that turn from that brilliant yellow to a blacky brown crispness through the gift of a charcoal burner.)

The chana, chickpeas, are cooked in a 'chola' a dome-like copper pot. Chana are never cooked in aluminium. Legend has it that choley in a copper pot will not turn bad whereas in any other vessel it will. The chickpeas are deeply flavoured and finished with freshly chopped tomato, onion, chilli and coriander... They taste of my childhood, of a thousand family meals.

Next stop is lunch. It's 3.30 pm but a boy has to eat! So it's to Sunil's Dhaba on the GT Road, 70 km short of Delhi from the east. I opt for a vegetarian lunch: dal makhani, malai paneer. India is probably the only country in the world where I could exist meaningfully as a non-meat eater; obviously avoiding the Mughal-inspired enclaves! I scoop mouthfuls of the paneer and dal with fresh, hot tandoori rotis. The kitchen is but a few feet away. This is the great joy of dhaba eating. No fancy linen, cutlery, crockery. Ceremony is more often kicked rather than stood upon. You can see what is being cooked and what is being cooked is what you are eating. And how did it taste? Comfort. Joy. Life. The taste of home, the taste of Punjab. Few dishes epitomise the quintessences of my forebears, the Punjabis, more than dal and roti. I know I'm getting closer to home...

DELHI

India's capital and the melting pot of Indian ethnic multiplicity. The city state of Delhi has been revamped for the 21st century, whilst maintaining its historical antecedents. Delhi is a microcosm for the rest of India; something from everywhere and something for everyone.

AMCHOORWALEY KARELA

Stuffed bitter gourd

SERVES 4

8 karela (bitter gourd)

½ teaspoon turmeric

I teaspoon salt

3 tablespoons vegetable oil

FOR THE FILLING

I potato, washed

60 g/2 oz raw unsalted peanuts, skinned

2 tablespoons vegetable oil

I teaspoon fennel seeds

2.5-cm/1-inch piece ginger, peeled and finely grated

2 green chillies, chopped

2 red onions, chopped

I teaspoon chilli powder

½ teaspoon turmeric

I teaspoon salt, or to taste

I tablespoon amchoor (dried mango powder)

½ teaspoon garam masala

juice of I lemon

few sprigs coriander, chopped

Peel the karela and then slit in half lengthways keeping the halves joined and remove the seeds. Chop the seeds and set aside.

Put the karela in a bowl and sprinkle with the turmeric and salt. Mix well, cover and leave to stand for I hour.

To make the filling, cook the potato in a saucepan of boiling water for about 20 minutes until just tender. Leave to cool, then peel and chop finely.

Heat a heavy-based frying pan and dry roast the peanuts, shaking the pan frequently, until golden brown. Leave to cool, then crush in a food processor or put in a double layer of plastic bags and bash with a rolling pin.

Heat the oil in a wok or large frying pan, add the fennel seeds and cook until they crackle. Add the ginger and chillies and sauté, stirring, for I minute. Add the onions and cook until golden brown. Stir in the chopped karela seeds, potato and peanuts and cook for 3–4 minutes. Add the chilli powder, turmeric and salt, mix well and cook for a further 2 minutes. Turn off the heat and mix in the amchoor, garam masala, lemon juice and chopped coriander. Leave to cool.

Stuff the karela with the filling mixture, then tie clean string around the karela to prevent the filling from coming out.

Heat the oil in a large non-stick frying pan, add the stuffed karela, then cover and cook over a low heat for about 12–15 minutes until crisp. Remove the string before serving.

Bhalla Papdi Chaat

Lentil dumplings with fried pastry, yoghurt and pomegranate seeds

SERVES 4

FOR THE DUMPLINGS

200 g/7 oz urad dal (white lentils)

2.5-cm/1-inch piece ginger, peeled and finely grated

2 green chillies, chopped

30 g/1¼ oz sultanas, chopped

1 teaspoon black pepper

pinch baking powder

1 teaspoon salt, or to taste

vegetable oil, for deep-frying

FOR THE PAPDI

180 g/6 oz plain flour

pinch salt

1 teaspoon carom seeds

2 tablespoons vegetable oil, plus extra for deep-frying

FOR THE YOGHURT

400 g/14 oz thick natural yoghurt

40 g/1½ oz granulated sugar

40 g/1½ oz runny honey

½ teaspoon salt, or to taste

100 g/3½ oz cooked chickpeas

1 teaspoon chilli powder

1 teaspoon amchoor (dried mango powder)

½ teaspoon ground cumin

few sprigs coriander, chopped

1 teaspoon salt, or to taste

Tamarind chutney (see page 133)

Mint and coriander chutney (see page 132)

2 tablespoons pomegranate seeds

First make the dumplings. Rinse the lentils under cold water running water, then drain and leave to soak in fresh cold water overnight. Drain the dal, put in a blender or food processor and blend to a thick smooth paste – try not to add any water, but if necessary, add a spoonful at a time so that the paste remains thick. Transfer the dal paste to a bowl, add the ginger, chillies, sultanas, crushed black peppercorns, baking powder and salt and mix well.

Heat enough oil for deep-frying in a wok or deep saucepan to 160°C/325°F, or until a cube of bread browns in about 60 seconds. Carefully drop tablespoonfuls of the mixture into the oil and deep-fry over a medium heat until golden brown. Remove and drain on kitchen paper. Immerse the fried dumplings in hot water for 2–3 minutes until soft, then drain and squeeze out any excess water. Leave to cool.

Now make the papdi. Sift the flour and salt into a large bowl, add the carom seeds and mix together, then stir in the oil. Make a well in the centre, add 80 ml/3 fl oz water and gradually mix in to make a firm dough. Knead until well combined, then cover and leave to stand for 30 minutes.

Meanwhile, for the yoghurt, put all the ingredients in a large bowl, add 125 ml/4 fl oz and whisk together until smooth. Cover and refrigerate until ready to serve the dish.

Divide the dough into 4 equal-sized pieces. Roll out each piece of dough thinly on a lightly floured surface, prick with a fork and then cut into small squares. Reheat the oil in the wok or saucepan to 180°C/350°F, or until a cube of bread browns in 30 seconds. Add the papdi, in batches, and deep-fry until crisp and golden brown. Remove with a slotted spoon, drain on kitchen paper and leave to cool.

To assemble, mix together the papdi, cooked chickpeas, chilli powder, amchoor, cumin, coriander and salt. Put the dumplings in a serving bowl, pour over a quarter of the yoghurt and neatly arrange the chickpea mixture on top, then pour over the remaining yoghurt. Spoon the chutneys on top of the yoghurt and scatter with the pomegranate seeds.

Kaleji Pao

Chicken liver masala with pao bread

SERVES 4

FOR THE PAO

15 g/½ oz fresh yeast

35 g/1¼ oz granulated sugar

500 g/1 lb 2 oz plain flour, plus extra for dusting

pinch salt

1 tablespoon vegetable oil

½ teaspoon chilli powder

¼ teaspoon ground cumin

¼ teaspoon dried fenugreek leaves, crumbled

¼ teaspoon garam masala

1 egg

2 tablespoons milk

1 tablespoon sunflower seeds

butter, for spreading

800 g/1 lb 12 oz chicken livers

40 g/1½ oz thick natural yoghurt

1 tablespoon ginger and garlic paste (see page 30)

1 teaspoon chilli powder

1 teaspoon salt, or to taste

2 tablespoons vegetable oil

6 cloves

2 cinnamon sticks

½ teaspoon caraway seeds

First make the pao. Blend the yeast with 100 ml/3½ fl oz tepid water and the sugar. Sift the flour and salt into a bowl and mix together, then stir in the oil, chilli powder, cumin, fenugreek leaves and garam masala. Make a well in the centre, add the yeast mixture and 175 ml/6 fl oz water and gradually mix in to make a soft dough.

Knead the dough on a lightly floured surface for a few minutes until firm, elastic and no longer sticky. Place in a large bowl, cover with a clean tea towel and leave to rise for about 45 minutes–1 hour or until doubled in size.

Turn out onto a lightly floured surface and knead well. Divide it into 70 g/2½ oz pieces and shape into rolls. Place the rolls on baking sheets, spacing them well apart. Cover with a clean damp tea towel and leave in a warm place to prove for about 1 hour until doubled in size. Preheat the oven to 220°C/425°F/gas 7.

Beat the egg with milk and brush over the tops of the rolls. Sprinkle with the sunflower seeds and bake in the oven for 15–20 minutes until golden. Remove from the oven and leave to cool.

While the rolls are baking and cooling, clean the livers by discarding any sinews and dark or green-looking parts. Rinse the livers under cold running water, then drain and pat dry with kitchen paper. Mix together the yoghurt, ginger and garlic paste, chilli powder and salt in a shallow dish, add the livers and turn to coat in the mixture. Cover and set aside while you cook the sauce.

Heat the oil in large frying pan, add the cloves and cinnamon and leave for a few minutes to allow their flavours to infuse the oil. Add the caraway seeds and cook until they crackle, then add the fenugreek leaves and cook for 1 minute. Add the onions and cook until soft and translucent. Stir in the ground coriander, cumin and tomatoes, cover and cook over a medium heat for about 5 minutes until the tomatoes are tender. Add the chicken livers and cook for 8–10 minutes.

½ bunch fresh fenugreek leaves

2 onions, chopped

1 teaspoon ground coriander

½ teaspoon ground cumin

2 tomatoes, sliced

1 teaspoon garam masala

juice of 1 lemon juice

few sprigs coriander, chopped

Meanwhile, cut the rolls in half horizontally, toast on a tawa or in a large non-stick frying pan and spread with butter.

Turn the heat off under the chicken liver masala, then sprinkle with the garam masala, squeeze over the lemon juice and scatter with the chopped coriander. Serve immediately with the pao.

Masala Chai

Spiced tea

SERVES 4

3 teaspoons English breakfast loose leaf tea

6 green cardamom pods

6 black peppercorns

4 cloves

1 cinnamon stick

2.5-cm/1-inch piece ginger, peeled and finely grated

250 ml/9 fl oz full-fat milk

sugar or jaggery, for sweetening

Bring 500 ml/18 fl oz water to the boil in a saucepan, add the tea, green cardamoms, black peppercorns, cloves, cinnamon and ginger and continue to simmer over a medium heat for 2 minutes.

Add the milk and simmer for a further 5 minutes. Remove from heat and stir in sugar or jaggery to taste. Strain through a fine sieve and serve hot.

Bhunna Chutney Paneer

Paneer with a sweet filling cooked in the tandoor

SERVES 4

1 kg/2 lb 4 oz paneer

melted butter, for basting

1 lemon, cut into wedges, to serve

FOR THE FILLING

vegetable oil, for deep-frying

100 g/3½ oz raw unsalted cashew nuts

100 g/3½ oz sultanas

50 g/1¾ oz sweet mango chutney

1 tablespoon Mint and coriander chutney (see page 133)

2.5-cm/1-inch piece ginger, peeled and finely grated

2 green chillies, chopped

few sprigs mint, chopped

1 teaspoon amchoor (dried mango powder)

½ teaspoon chilli powder

¼ teaspoon ground cumin

1 teaspoon salt, or to taste

FOR THE MARINADE

4 teaspoons mustard oil

½ teaspoon turmeric

200 g/7 oz hung yoghurt (see page 218)

1 teaspoon chilli powder

½ teaspoon carom seeds

½ teaspoon dried fenugreek leaves, crumbled

½ teaspoon garam masala

1 teaspoon salt, or to taste

Cut the paneer into 4-cm/1½-inch cubes. Slice each paneer cube in half horizontally but without cutting right through so that they can be stuffed.

To make the filling, heat enough oil for deep-frying in a wok or deep saucepan to 180–190°C/350°–375°F, or until a cube of bread browns in 30 seconds. Add the cashew nuts and sultanas and deep-fry until golden brown. Remove with a slotted spoon and drain on kitchen paper, then roughly chop.

Mix together the sweet mango and Mint and coriander chutneys, ginger, chillies, mint, amchoor, chilli powder, cumin and salt. Add the fried cashew nuts and sultanas and mix well. Stuff the paneer cubes with the filling mixture and set aside.

Now make the marinade. Mix the oil and turmeric together thoroughly in a bowl. Add the yoghurt, chilli powder, carom seeds, fenugreek, garam masala and salt and mix well. Add the stuffed paneer cubes and mix gently so that all the cubes are evenly covered with the marinade.

Thread the paneer cubes onto metal skewers and cook in a medium tandoor or over a barbecue, or on a baking sheet in a preheated oven at 160°C/325°F/gas 3, for 5–6 minutes, turning halfway through and basting with melted butter. Serve hot with lemon wedges.

DELHI

FRANK ZAPPA WROTE A SONG CALLED 'CITY OF TINY LIGHTS'. I think he must have been inspired by a drive into Delhi at dusk. Delhi is atwinkle with a million tiny lights as I wend my way wearily through the cold and the evening traffic. There's something intrinsically wrong about feeling a chill in India.

I love Delhi. I love Delhi because my dad loves Delhi. He was a customs officer in the city some fifty years ago. He would cut about the city on a Vespa in the sharpest suits and smoothest turbans having the best adventures. I drive into the city in a beaten up van, wearing too much Adidas and wrapped in a shawl, awash with my day's eating. I share none of his elegance. But we have adventure in common.

By morning a moribund mist sits over an unseasonably cold New Delhi. An army of attache-case carrying citizens convey themselves to worlds of paper and pen. I eschew the present and prefer the past.

Where there is the New there must have been the Old. New Delhi is the sprawling international capital, home to diplomats, bureaucrats and some of India's super-rich. New Delhi is the gateway to modern, vibrant, cosmopolitan India. Proud, wide boulevards, stunning modern architecture, manicured gardens. New Delhi is the establishment. Old Delhi... well, that is another story.

The Old Town is the polar opposite of New Delhi. Instead of the wide, tree-lined boulevards and the majesty of space, the Old Town is a morass of the random; chowks and gullies, nooks and crannies. People live on top of each other and the buildings themselves barely remember their once glory days.

Chandi Chowk is where everyone eventually ends up or passes through. The word pandemonium seems somehow insufficient to convey the atmosphere on Chandi. It's like one of those modern dance pieces where a troupe of performers wander aimlessly and messily around the stage only to come together in a precise choreographed moment of vision. But Chandi Chowk is choreographer-free. My reluctant autorickshaw-wallah tackles the complexity en route to Paratha ki Gully, a squiggling alleyway devoted to the joyous paratha. A left and a right turn away from the madness, the constant flow of life and bikes and scooters and carts, Paratha Ki Gully is an oasis of calm; calm and carbohydrate. Tea first. I find a tiny courtyard, fashioned around a Peepul tree. The tree itself has become a mini-Mandir... deities scattered in and amongst the complex root structure. And in the

lightless shade sits a chai wallah. This is the sort of place you would never happen upon; this place requires prior knowledge, which luckily I have. This is said to be one of the finest cups of tea in the Old Town, moments from the GT Road.

Operating on the steps of a basement doorway the chai wallah looks like he has been here as long as India has been in existence. Half his body hidden underground, he pounds, counts, stirs, strains and starts all over again.

The pot itself is a story of hours, days, weeks, months and years of almost constant chai making. In the thirty minutes I'm here the pot seldom rests.

It's ironic to be in Paratha ki Gully and not be hunting out paratha. But I know that I'm heading to the Punjab, conveyed down the GT Road, where parathas are in plentiful supply.

I'm after a famous North India street snack, dal ki kachori. Kachori is a deep-fried bread, in this instance filled with chana dal. It's served alongside aloo ki sabzi (potato curry), and a zingy carrot pickle. It's food that is easily eaten on the go, one-handed eating at its best. Like all the best convenience food, there is an internal balance to all the flavours and tastes in dal ki kachori. I like the idea that there is a food Darwinism that evolves with street food like this; only the fittest ingredients survive allowing for the instant hit of taste and belly-filling deliciousness. I walk as I eat and I eat as I walk.

And whilst I'm not scheduled to eat paratha in the gully, the Punjabi in me realises the international crime of being here and not eating paratha: it's a sin that can never be forgiven. I wander further down the alley, my hands still smeared with the scent of chickpeas and potatoes and pickle. I am surrounded by yet more food and find a small shop that apparently makes great paratha. Such a pressure, serving food in business that is made by every mother in the land. Why would anyone eat a second-rate paratha outside when mum's are so brilliant?

My mum makes astonishingly good mooli ki paratha and gobi ki paratha. Mooli is such a Punjabi vegetable. Omnipresent in every salad, its mustardy crunchiness is the perfect sharpener before a meal. (Punjabis eat salad before the meal is served; we're weird that way.) I must have been the only child in the west of Scotland that craved gobi; I love cauliflower. And it is this very love, a love undimmed, undiminished by age that leads me to this altar of metal and glass and PVC: I shall eat paratha.

Freshly made mooli paratha followed by a spiced cauliflower paratha. The unmistakeable flavour of ghee, clarified butter, is omnipresent, an unwelcome reminder to my arteries of their continued hardening! Paradise is silence and a full stomach. Silence, a full stomach and the thought of an onward journey to the heart of the Punjab. It would seem that for this man, at any rate, the way to his stomach will be through his heart.

TANGDI

Marinated chicken legs

SERVES 4

8 chicken legs, skinned

2 tablespoons ginger and
garlic paste (see page 30)

juice of 1 lemon

1 teaspoon salt, or to taste

FOR THE PASTE

160 g/5¾ oz hung yoghurt
(see page 218)

1 teaspoon garam masala

2 tablespoons mustard oil

1 teaspoon chilli powder

½ teaspoon dried fenugreek
leaves, crumbled

Rinse the chicken legs under cold running water, then drain and pat dry with kitchen paper.

Mix together the ginger and garlic paste, lemon juice and salt in a shallow non-metallic dish. Add the chicken legs and turn to coat in the mixture, then cover and leave to marinate at cool room temperature for 20 minutes.

Put all the paste ingredients in a bowl and mix together well. Add to the chicken and turn to coat in the paste, then cover and leave to marinate in the fridge for 4–5 hours.

Thread the chicken onto metal skewers and cook in a hot tandoor or over a barbecue, turning frequently, for about 10 minutes or until cooked through.

PUDINEY KE TIKKEY

Barbecued chicken with green herbs

SERVES 4

8 skinless chicken breasts

2 limes

2 tablespoons ginger and garlic paste (see page 30)

1 teaspoon salt, or to taste

1 teaspoon garam masala

FOR THE HERB PASTE

1 bunch mint, roughly chopped

1 bunch coriander, roughly chopped

6 cloves garlic, roughly chopped

5 green chillies, roughly chopped

5-cm/2-inch piece ginger, peeled and roughly chopped

2 tablespoons thick natural yoghurt

3 tablespoons vegetable oil

Cut each chicken breast in half lengthways. Rinse under cold running water, then drain and pat dry with kitchen paper.

Grate the zest of the limes and set aside to use in the herb paste. Squeeze the juice from the limes and mix with the ginger and garlic paste and salt in a shallow non-metallic dish. Add the chicken and turn to coat in the mixture, then cover and leave to marinate at cool room temperature for 20 minutes.

Meanwhile, to make the herb paste, blend the lime zest with all the other paste ingredients in a blender or food processor to a smooth paste.

Add the herb paste to the marinated chicken and mix together well, then sprinkle over the garam masala. Thread the chicken onto metal skewers and cook in a hot tandoor or over a barbecue, turning frequently, for about 4–5 minutes each side, or until cooked through.

Shahi Korma

Delhi-style lamb curry cooked in a sealed pot

SERVES 4

1½ kg/2 lb 4 oz mutton
on the bone, cut into large
chunks (or use lamb or goat)

vegetable oil, for deep-frying

3 onions, sliced

300 g/10½ oz thick natural
yoghurt

100 g/3½ oz ghee

3 tablespoons ground
coriander

2 tablespoons chilli powder

8 black peppercorns

6 green cardamom pods

4 black cardamom pods

5 cloves

1 teaspoon cumin seeds

2 tablespoons ginger and
garlic paste (see page 30)

1 teaspoon garam masala

¼ teaspoon ground mace

¼ teaspoon ground nutmeg

1 teaspoon salt, or to taste

Rinse the meat under cold running water, then drain and pat dry with kitchen paper.

Heat enough oil for deep-frying in a wok or deep saucepan to 180–190°C/350°–375°F, or until a cube of bread browns in 30 seconds. Deep-fry the onions until golden brown. Remove with a slotted spoon and drain on kitchen paper.

Put the meat in a large heavy-based lidded flameproof casserole or saucepan, add all the remaining ingredients and mix well. Stir in the fried onions and enough cold water to cover the meat, then cover and cook over a low heat, stirring regularly at intervals, for 1½ hours until the meat is very tender.

DAL MAKHANI

Black lentil dal

SERVES 4

300 g/10½ oz urad dal (whole black lentils)

100 g/3½ oz chana dal (yellow split peas)

100 g/3½ oz dried crab-eye beans

50 g/1¾ oz butter, diced

¼ teaspoon ground asafoetida, mixed with a little cold water

5-cm/2-inch piece ginger, peeled and cut into julienne

2 teaspoons chilli powder

1 teaspoon salt, or to taste

50 ml/2 fl oz single cream

2 green chillies, slit lengthways

1 teaspoon garam masala

FOR THE TOMATO SAUCE

1.25 kg/2 lb 12 oz tomatoes on the vine

4 green chillies

1 teaspoons chilli powder

3 teaspoons oil

salt, to taste

Rinse the lentils, chana dal and crab-eye beans under cold running water, then drain and leave to soak in fresh cold water overnight.

Drain the pulses and put in a large saucepan with plenty of cold water. Bring to the boil and cook for about 1½-2 hours, or until tender.

To make the tomato sauce, wash and cut the tomatoes in half and then place in a large heavy-based saucepan. Add the chillies, chilli powder and 2 teaspoons of vegetable oil. Add 120 ml/4 fl oz water and cook over a medium heat for 20–30 minutes, stirring from time to time, or until the tomatoes are soft and pulpy. Allow to cool and then blend in a food processor or blender and then pass through a sieve. Return to the pan, add 1 teaspoon of oil and salt to taste and bring to the boil again. Turn off the heat.

Drain the cooked pulses, return to the pan and add the tomato sauce, butter, asafoetida mixture, ginger, chilli powder, tomato purée and salt. Cook for a further 20–25 minutes.

Stir in the cream, chillies and garam masala before serving.

SAUNTH KI CHUTNEY

Tamarind chutney

SERVES 4

500 g/1 lb 2 oz tamarind

1 kg/2 lb 4 oz jaggery

100 g/3½ dried dates, stoned

3 tablespoons ground fennel

2 tablespoons ground cumin

1 tablespoon chilli powder

1 tablespoon freshly ground black pepper

1 teaspoon ground ginger

½ teaspoon black salt

salt, to taste

Soak the tamarind, jaggery and dates separately in warm water for at least 2 hours. Press the tamarind through a sieve to extract the pulp, discarding the liquid. Drain the jaggery and dates.

Put the tamarind pulp, jaggery and dates in a heavy-based saucepan, add about 1 litre/1¾ pints water and cook over a medium heat for 25–30 minutes.

Add the fennel, cumin, chilli powder and black pepper, mix well and cook for a further 10–15 minutes or until the mixture is thick. Mix in the ginger, black salt and salt to taste and cook for 2–3 minutes.

Leave to cool and then strain and store in an airtight container.

HAREE CHUTNEY

Mint and coriander chutney

SERVES 4

2 bunches mint

1 bunch coriander

handful spinach leaves (preferably young)

2.5-cm/1-inch piece ginger, peeled

6 cloves garlic, peeled

2 green chillies

3 tablespoons natural yoghurt

1 teaspoon amchoor (dried mango powder)

1 teaspoon ground cumin

1 teaspoon salt, or to taste

juice of 1 lemon

Rinse the mint, coriander and spinach under cold running water, then drain.

Roughly chop the ginger, garlic and chillies. Put in a blender or food processor with the herbs, spinach and yoghurt and blend to a smooth paste, adding a little water if necessary.

Transfer the chutney to a bowl, add the amchoor, cumin and salt and mix well. Squeeze in the lemon juice, mix again and check the seasoning. Store in an airtight container in the fridge. Use within two days.

Gobhi Shalgum ka Achar

Cauliflower and turnip pickle

SERVES 4

1 cauliflower

4 carrots

250 g/9 oz baby turnips

½ teaspoon chilli powder

½ teaspoon turmeric

½ teaspoon ground coriander

1 teaspoon salt, or to taste

FOR THE MASALA

2 tomatoes

300 ml/10 fl oz mustard oil

2 onions, very finely chopped

1 tablespoon ginger and garlic paste (see page 30)

1½ teaspoons chilli powder

2 teaspoons ground coriander

1 teaspoon turmeric

1 teaspoon salt, or to taste

4 teaspoons whole panch phoran (see page 210), crushed

3 teaspoons black mustard seeds, crushed

Cut the cauliflower into florets, the carrots into batons and the turnips into thick rounds. Put the vegetables in a bowl, add the chilli powder, turmeric, coriander and salt and mix well.

Spread the vegetables out on a baking tray and place in a very low oven for about 1½ hours, or leave in a cooling oven with the door open overnight.

To make the masala, blend the tomatoes in a blender or food processor to a smooth purée. Heat the oil in a wok or large frying pan, add the onions and cook until golden brown. Add the ginger and garlic paste and cook, stirring, for 2 minutes. Add the chilli powder, coriander, turmeric and salt and cook, stirring, for a further 2 minutes.

Add the puréed tomatoes and cook until all the liquid has evaporated and the oil separates. Add the crushed panch phoran and mustard seeds and mix well. Turn off the heat and leave the mixture to cool. When it is just warm, add the vegetables and mix well.

Store the pickle in an airtight container in a warm place or in the sun and leave to mature for 2–3 days before eating. Store for up to one week.

KASHMIR

Strictly speaking, Kashmir is not on the actual GT Road. The Grand Trunk bends away west skirting through the Punjab and heading into modern day Afghanistan. But that doesn't mean the food of Kashmir isn't present on this stretch of the road. The harsh reality is that the troubled, divided state has sent refugees and emissaries in every direction, seeking peace and fleeing war. Delhi has a few Kashmiri stalls by the GT and through Punjab a few more spring up.

MY UNCLE, LIKE ANI'S, served in Kashmir as an Army Officer. I remember vividly the eight-hour ascent from Jammu station to Srinagar where my aunt, uncle and cousins lived. I can have been no more than ten years old as our jeep conveyed us in ever decreasing circles higher up the foothills of the Himalayas. Halfway through the drive we stopped for a break and a little sustenance. This was to be the first time I fell in love; albeit with food.

A handful of shacks nestled together, huddling over a sheer drop of hundreds of feet; the narrowness and disrepair of the road offered little comfort to what had already been a perilous journey.

One of these run-down shacks was teeming with life, clearly the most popular by some way. Out front a man sat with three cauldrons. I watched him dish up: a steel plate was adorned with bright white rice from the largest cauldron. Upon this was lovingly spooned a ladle and a half of rajmah, curried kidney beans. The final cauldron, the smallest of the three, held ghee, clarified butter, which was delicately placed into a small well in the rajmah. Paradise on a plate.

I wanted nothing more at that point in my life that the tricolore joy that that plate promised. But this was India in 1979; there was no way on God's earth that my dad was going to let me eat from a street stall. No way. Instead a can of Fanta and a bag of crisps tried in vain to satiate the unsatiable. I almost cried with frustration.

But romance seldom dies. Thirty years later I was making the same journey, making the self-same stop. And there it was. The shack. The memory. The frustration. The rajmah. This time I was the architect of my own future. I paused a moment, in quiet reflection upon my lovely dad, before piling into a plate of curried kidney beans. It was more delicious than I had imagined for three decades. And in that moment everything in the world seemed good, right and proper.

KABARGAH

Fried lamb ribs Kashmiri-style

SERVES 4

500 g/1 lb 2 oz lamb ribs

400 ml/14 fl oz full-fat milk

6 cloves

3 green cardamom pods

3 bay leaves

1 cinnamon stick

pinch saffron threads

2 teaspoons ground fennel

1 teaspoon ground ginger

¼ teaspoon ground asafoetida

1 teaspoon salt

70 g/2½ oz chickpea flour

100 g/3½ oz thick natural yoghurt

1 teaspoon chilli powder

vegetable oil, for deep-frying

Rinse the ribs under cold running water, then drain and pat dry with kitchen paper. Put in a large, heavy-based saucepan or flameproof casserole with the milk, cloves, cardamom pods, bay leaves, cinnamon stick, saffron, fennel, ginger, asafoetida and 1 teaspoon salt or to taste. Stir in 475 ml/17 fl oz cold water, bring to the boil and then simmer for about 30 minutes until the ribs are tender and the liquid has evaporated, stirring occasionally to prevent sticking. Leave to cool.

Mix together the chickpea flour, yoghurt, chilli powder and salt to taste in a bowl, then beat in enough water to make a batter that is the right consistency just to coat the ribs; neither too thick nor too thin. Beat thoroughly until smooth.

Heat enough oil for deep-frying in a wok or deep saucepan to 180–190°C/350°–375°F, or until a cube of bread browns in 30 seconds. Dip the ribs in the batter to coat, add to the hot oil, in batches, and deep-fry until golden brown. Remove and drain on kitchen paper. Keep the cooked ribs hot while frying the remainder.

Serve with a salad of cucumber, tomato and red onion and Mint and coriander chutney (see page 133).

ROGAN JOSH

Spicy lamb curry

SERVES 4

1 kg/2 lb 4 oz lean boneless lamb, cut into 2.5-cm/1-inch chunks

4 tablespoons vegetable oil

2 black cardamom pods

4 green cardamom pods

4 cloves

2 bay leaves

1 cinnamon stick

2 onions, chopped

2 tablespoons ginger and garlic paste (see page 30)

2 teaspoons chilli powder

1 teaspoon ground coriander

$^1/_2$ teaspoon turmeric

4 tomatoes, puréed

100 g/3$^1/_2$ oz thick natural yoghurt

1 teaspoon salt, or to taste

1 teaspoon garam masala

few sprigs coriander, chopped

Rinse the lamb under cold running water, then drain and pat dry with kitchen paper.

Heat the oil in a large, heavy-based frying pan. Add the whole spices and leave over a gentle heat for a few minutes to allow their flavours to infuse the oil.

Add the onions to the pan and cook until golden brown, then add the lamb and cook over a high heat until well seared all over. Add the ginger and garlic paste and cook, stirring frequently, for 2 minutes. Stir in 500–600 ml/17–20 fl oz water and simmer gently for about 30 minutes, adding more water if necessary. Stir in the ground spices and cook for a further 15 minutes.

Add the puréed tomatoes and yoghurt and cook for a further 15 minutes, or until the lamb is cooked through and tender. Season to taste and then sprinkle with the garam masala and scatter over the chopped coriander before serving.

GHUSTABEY

Pounded lamb dumplings in a
yoghurt and fennel sauce

SERVES 4

1 kg/2 lb 4 oz boneless
lamb, diced

125 g/4¹/₂ oz lamb fat, diced

1 teaspoon ground fennel

¹/₂ teaspoon ground ginger

1 teaspoon salt, or to taste

3 green chillies, chopped

few sprigs coriander, chopped

FOR THE SAUCE

1 kg/2 lb 4 oz thick natural
yoghurt

2 teaspoons ground fennel

1 teaspoon ground ginger

1 teaspoon salt, or to taste

75 ml/2¹/₂ fl oz mustard oil

5 bay leaves

¹/₄ teaspoon ground asafoetida

2 tablespoons ginger and
garlic paste (see page 30)

Put the lamb, lamb fat, fennel, ginger, salt, chillies and coriander in a large bowl and mix together well. Transfer to a food processor and process to a fine paste.

Divide the paste into 12 equal-sized portions, then roll each portion into a ball. Set aside.

To make the sauce, mix together the yoghurt, fennel, ginger and salt in a bowl, then whisk in about 1–1.2 litres/1³/₄–2 pints water.

Heat the oil in a heavy-based saucepan, add the bay leaves and asafoetida and cook for 20 seconds. Add the ginger and garlic paste and cook, stirring, for 1 minute. Add the yoghurt mixture and bring to the boil, stirring continuously. Add the dumplings and gently simmer for about 45 minutes until cooked through and tender.

Note Traditionally, the lamb mixture is pounded with a ghustabey hammer for at least an hour before the required consistency is achieved, but a food processor achieves a comparable result. Ghustaba is served as the last course of the Kashmiri Wazvan banquet as it helps in digestion because of the fennel and ginger in it.

Kadam ka Saag

Kashmiri greens stir-fry

SERVES 4

500 g/1 lb 2 oz kohlrabi
leaves

1 tablespoon mustard oil

2 dried red chillies

2 green chillies, slit
lengthways

½ teaspoon ground asafoetida

½ teaspoon turmeric

1 teaspoon salt, or to taste

Chop the kohlrabi leaves, rinse under cold running water and drain well.

Heat the oil in a wok or large frying pan, add the dried red chillies, green chillies and asafoetida and cook, stirring, for 1 minute. Add the kohlrabi leaves, turmeric and salt to taste and cook, stirring, for 2–3 minutes.

Add 350 ml/12 fl oz water and gently simmer over a low heat until the leaves are tender and any liquid has evaporated.

KAHWA

Kashmiri-style tea

SERVES 4

4 teaspoons Kashmiri green tea or other loose green tea

pinch saffron threads

¼ teaspoon ground green cardamom

¼ teaspoon ground cinnamon

4 teaspoons skinned almonds

granulated sugar, for sweetening

Bring 400 ml/14 fl oz water to the boil in a saucepan. Add the tea, saffron, cardamom and cinnamon and leave to infuse for about 5 minutes.

Crush the almonds lightly in a pestle and mortar or pulse briefly in a food processor. Add a teaspoonful of the almonds to each cup, then pour over the tea, sweeten with sugar to taste and serve.

North West Frontier Province & Afghanistan

The GT road was no doubt integral to the Sikh colonisation of Afghanistan and nowhere on the road is the geography more pronounced in the food available.

THE BARREN, harsh, extreme climate of Afghanistan and the North West Frontier Province means that few things can be grown or farmed. The hardy goat can survive and wheat can be grown. It's a simple yet delicious diet; none of the Moghul excesses of cream and nuts, none of the abundant vegetables of the Punjab. Meat and bread: that is the Kabul way. But what meat, what breads. And Kabul is the end of the GT Road, a road that recent travellers have used to escape the decades of conflict in Afghanistan. An unstable Afghanistan has meant the movement of people. And with the people came their food.

Baigan ka Raita

Chilled yoghurt and aubergine raita

SERVES 4

250 g/9 oz Greek-style yoghurt

salt, to taste

1 large aubergine

½ teaspoon turmeric

6 tablespoons vegetable oil

1 tablespoon cumin seeds

Whisk the yoghurt with about 50 ml/2 fl oz water in a bowl to loosen it a bit, then add salt to taste and mix well.

Trim the aubergine, then cut into thin rounds. Place in a shallow dish, sprinkle with the turmeric and salt to taste and set aside for 5 minutes.

Heat the oil in a large frying pan, add the aubergine slices and cook over a medium-high heat for about 2 minutes on each side, or until golden brown. Remove the fried aubergine with a fish slice and place on top of the yoghurt.

Add the cumin seeds to the remaining oil in the pan and cook until they crackle, then pour the seeds and oil over the yoghurt and aubergine. Stir well, leave to cool, then cover and chill before serving.

CHAPLI KEBAB

Griddled lamb mince kebabs

SERVES 4

600 g/1 lb 5 oz boneless lamb, cut into 2-cm/¾-inch chunks

5-cm/2-inch piece ginger, peeled and diced

10 cloves garlic

4 green chillies

1 bunch coriander

1 bunch mint

1 tablespoon chilli powder

1 teaspoon salt, or to taste

2 red onions, chopped

1 teaspoon garam masala

1 teaspoon crushed black peppercorns

1 egg, beaten

juice of 1 lemon

1 tomato, sliced

2 tablespoons vegetable oil

Put the lamb, ginger, garlic, chillies, herbs, chilli powder and salt in a large bowl and mix together well. Pass the lamb mixture through a mincer to make a coarse mince.

Add the onions, garam masala, crushed black peppercorns and egg and mix well. Squeeze in the lemon juice and mix again.

Divide the mixture into 8 equal-sized portions, then flatten and shape each portion into a round patty about 5 mm/¼ inch thick. Press a slice of tomato into one side of each patty.

Heat the oil in a large non-stick frying pan, add the patties and cook over a medium-high heat for about 3–4 minutes on each side until well browned and cooked through.

Ajwaini Bhindi

Okra stir-fried with carom seeds

SERVES 4

500 g/1 lb 2 oz okra

2 tablespoons vegetable oil

½ teaspoon carom seeds

2 mild green chillies, chopped

5-cm/2-inch piece ginger, peeled and cut into julienne

2 red onions, chopped

½ tablespoon ground coriander

1 teaspoon chilli powder

¼ teaspoon turmeric

1 teaspoon salt, or to taste

4 tomatoes, chopped

1 tablespoon amchoor (dried mango powder)

juice of 1 lemon

Rinse the okra under cold running water, then drain and pat dry with kitchen paper. Cut into 2.5-cm/1-inch pieces.

Heat the oil in a wok or large frying pan, add the carom seeds, green chillies and ginger julienne and sauté for 2–3 minutes, then add the onions and cook until soft and translucent. Add the okra and cook, stirring, for a few minutes over a medium heat. Cover and cook over a low heat for about 5 minutes.

Add the coriander, chilli powder, turmeric and salt, cover and cook for 2 minutes, then stir in the tomatoes, cover and cook for another few minutes until the okra is tender. Stir in the amchoor and squeeze over the lemon juice before serving.

PENDA

Chicken korma served on roti

SERVES 4

2 whole poussins, each cut into 4 pieces

120 ml/4 fl oz vegetable oil

4 cinnamon sticks

8 cloves garlic, chopped

1 large onion, chopped

9 tomatoes, puréed

1 tablespoon chilli powder

¾ tablespoon ground coriander

¾ tablespoon turmeric

1 teaspoon ground cumin

1 teaspoon garam masala

1 teaspoon salt, or to taste

2 potatoes, peeled and halved

FOR THE ROTI

700 g/1 lb 9 oz self-raising flour, plus extra for dusting

1 teaspoon salt

250 ml/9 fl oz milk

Start by making the roti dough. Sift the flour and salt into a large bowl and mix together. Make a well in the centre, add the milk and 1.2 litres/2 pints water and gradually mix in to make a soft dough. Cover with a clean damp tea towel and leave to stand for 30 minutes.

Meanwhile, make the coriander chutney. Discard the coriander stems, then rinse the leaves under cold running water and pat dry with kitchen paper. Put in a blender or food processor with all the other chutney ingredients and blend to a fine paste. Check the seasoning, then set aside until ready to serve.

Divide the roti dough into 8 equal-sized pieces. Roll out each piece of dough on a lightly floured surface into a very thin round. Heat a tawa or large non-stick frying pan over a medium-high heat, add the roti, one at a time, and cook for 2 minutes on each side until lightly browned. Set aside.

Rinse the poussin pieces under cold running water, then drain and pat dry with kitchen paper. Heat the oil in a wok or large frying pan, add the cinnamon, garlic and onion and cook until the onion is golden brown. Add the poussin pieces, puréed tomatoes, chilli powder, coriander, turmeric, cumin, garam masala and salt and mix well. Stir in the potatoes and 1 litre/1¾ pints water. Cover and cook over a medium heat for about 20 minutes or until the poussin and potatoes are cooked through and tender.

FOR THE CORIANDER CHUTNEY

1 bunch coriander

5-cm/2-inch piece ginger, peeled and roughly chopped

8 cloves garlic, roughly chopped

6 green chillies, roughly chopped

1 onion, roughly chopped

3 tomatoes

100 g/3½ oz natural yoghurt

juice of 1 lemon

½ teaspoon salt, or to taste

FOR THE TARKA

2 tablespoons vegetable oil

4 cloves garlic, chopped

1 onion, chopped

1 teaspoon chilli powder

4 tomatoes, puréed

1 teaspoon salt, or to taste

While the poussin and potatoes are cooking, make the tarka. Heat the oil in a frying pan, add the garlic and onion and cook until the onion is golden brown. Stir in the chilli powder, puréed tomatoes and salt and then cook for about 5 minutes until the tomatoes are tender and the oil separates. Keep warm.

Remove the chicken and potatoes with a slotted spoon and set aside, then add 1 litre/1¾ pints water to the sauce in the pan and bring to the boil.

To assemble the dish, tear the roti into bite-sized pieces and place in a layer in the base of a deep serving dish. Pour the sauce over the roti layer so that it reaches the sides of the dish, completely covering the roti. Arrange the chicken and potatoes on top, then serve with the tarka and coriander chutney.

BEHARI KEBAB

Beef kebabs with poppy and sesame seeds

SERVES 4

1 kg/2 lb 4 oz striploin of beef (boneless sirloin)

80 ml/3 fl oz mustard oil

2 tablespoons ginger and garlic paste (see page 30)

1 teaspoon salt, or to taste

4 teaspoons vegetable oil

12 red chillies

2 tablespoons poppy seeds

2 tablespoons sesame seeds

1 teaspoon cumin seeds

2 tablespoons desiccated coconut

2 tablespoons garam masala

150 g/5½ oz natural yoghurt

Mint and coriander chutney (see page 133), to serve

Cut the beef into thin slices about 5–7.5 cm/2–3 inches wide and 10 cm/4 inches long. Mix together the mustard oil, ginger and garlic paste and salt in a shallow dish. Add the beef, turn to coat in the mixture, then cover and leave to marinate in the fridge for at least 2 hours.

Heat the vegetable oil in a large frying pan, add the chillies and fry until lightly browned. Remove and drain on kitchen paper. Leave to cool.

Grind the poppy, sesame and cumin seeds, desiccated coconut and fried red chilli in a spice or coffee grinder or with a pestle and mortar to a fine powder.

Mix together the spice powder, garam masala and yoghurt, add to the beef and mix well. Cover and leave to marinate in the fridge for about 8 hours.

Thread the meat onto metal skewers and cook over a low-medium barbecue, turning frequently, for about 6 minutes or until cooked through. Serve hot with Mint and coriander chutney.

CHICKEN BIRYANI

Chicken with basmati rice

SERVES 4

500 g/1 lb 2 oz basmati rice

vegetable oil, for frying

3 onions, sliced

2 poussin, each cut into 4 pieces

1 teaspoon caraway seeds

2 tablespoons ginger and garlic paste (see page 30)

1 tablespoon chilli powder

1 tablespoon ground coriander

1 tablespoon garam masala

1 teaspoon salt, or to taste

200 g/7oz thick natural yoghurt

2 teaspoons kewra water

8 stoned prunes

4 black cardamom pods

3 bay leaves

2 cinnamon sticks

7 green chillies, slit lengthways

few sprigs mint, chopped

1 lemon, sliced

1/2 teaspoon ground green cardamom

1/2 teaspoon saffron threads, soaked in a little hot water for 20 minutes

Rinse the rice in several changes of cold water until the water runs clear, then leave to soak in warm water for at least 1 hour.

Meanwhile, heat enough oil for deep-frying in a wok or deep saucepan to 180–190°C/350°–375°F, or until a cube of bread browns in 30 seconds. Add the onions and deep-fry until golden brown. Remove with a slotted spoon and drain on kitchen paper.

Skin the poussin pieces, rinse under cold running water, then drain and pat dry with kitchen paper. Heat 50 ml/2 fl oz oil in the wok or a large frying pan, add the caraway seeds and leave over a gentle heat for a few minutes to allow their flavour to infuse the oil. Stir in a quarter of the fried onions and the poussin pieces and cook over a high heat for 2–3 minutes until the chicken is well seared all over. Add the ginger and garlic paste and cook, stirring frequently, for 5 minutes. Add the chilli powder, coriander, garam masala and salt and mix well.

Whisk the remaining fried onions into the yoghurt and add to the pan, then cover and cook over a low heat for about 12–15 minutes until the chicken is almost cooked. Add the kewra water and prunes and cook for a further minute, then turn off the heat and set aside.

Bring a saucepan of water to the boil with the black cardamoms, bay leaves and cinnamon. Drain the rice, add to the boiling water and cook for about 5 minutes until half cooked. Drain. Preheat the oven to 180°C/350°F/gas 4.

Place three-quarters of the rice in a layer over the base of a large casserole, spread the chicken mixture on top, then add the chillies, chopped mint, lemon slices and ground cardamom. Cover with the remaining rice and sprinkle over the saffron and its soaking water. Cover with the lid and cook in the oven for 10 minutes. Gently mix the chicken and rice together before serving.

MANTU

Afghani-style steamed lamb dumplings with yoghurt

SERVES 4

FOR THE DOUGH

500 g/1 lb 2 oz plain flour, plus extra for dusting

1 teaspoon salt

2 eggs, beaten

FOR THE FILLING

7 cloves garlic, peeled

3 green chillies

2 tablespoons vegetable oil

500 g/1 lb 2 oz lamb mince

1 teaspoon salt, or to taste

1 teaspoon crushed black peppercorns

2 red onions, chopped

FOR THE SAUCE

4 teaspoons vegetable oil

2 cloves garlic, chopped

1 green chilli, chopped

1/2 small onion, chopped

200 g/7 oz lamb mince

3 tomatoes, chopped

1 green pepper, deseeded and roughly chopped

1 teaspoon salt, or to taste

1 teaspoon crushed black peppercorns

few sprigs mint, to garnish

First make the dough. Sift the flour and salt into a bowl and mix together. Make a well in the centre, add the eggs and 75–100 ml/2–3 fl oz water and gradually mix in. Knead to make a smooth dough. Wrap in clingfilm and place in the fridge to rest for at least 1½ hours.

Meanwhile, to make the filling, pound the garlic and chillies together with a pestle and mortar until well crushed. Heat the oil in a wok or large frying pan, add the crushed garlic and chillies and fry until golden. Add the lamb mince and cook, breaking it up with a wooden spoon, until browned. Add the salt and crushed black peppercorns and continue to cook for 5–7 minutes, stirring frequently to prevent the meat from sticking or burning. Transfer to a bowl, leave to cool, then stir in the onions.

To make the sauce, heat the oil in the pan, add the garlic, chilli and onion and sauté until the onion is soft and translucent. Add the lamb mince and cook, breaking it up with a wooden spoon, until browned. Add the tomatoes and green pepper and cook for about 10 minutes. Add the salt and crushed black peppercorns and cook for 1–2 minutes. Set aside until ready to reheat just before serving.

Divide the dough into 12 equal-sized pieces. Roll out each piece on a lightly floured surface to a round about 5 mm/¼ inch thick. Place 1½ tablespoons of the filling in the centre of one round. Take the two opposite corners and seal them together with your dampened fingers. Repeat with the remaining two corners, then pinch the adjacent corners together to create a parcel. Continue in the same way with the remaining dough and filling. Place the dumplings in a steamer and cook for 10 minutes.

FOR THE YOGHURT

150 g/5½ oz natural yoghurt

4 cloves garlic, grated

½ teaspoon salt, or to taste

Mix the yoghurt with the grated garlic and salt, then spread a layer over the base of a serving platter. Arrange the lamb parcels over the yoghurt, add another teaspoon of the yoghurt on the top of each parcel, then spoon the hot sauce over and garnish with mint sprigs.

BOULANI

Mini Afghani breads filled
with spring onion

SERVES 4

FOR THE DOUGH

10 g/¼ oz fresh yeast

500 g/1 lb 2 oz white plain
flour, plus extra for dusting

250 g/9 oz wholemeal plain
flour

1 teaspoon salt, or to taste

2 tablespoons vegetable oil,
plus extra for frying

FOR THE FILLING

2 bunches spring onions

1 teaspoon salt

1 teaspoon chilli powder

2 green chillies, chopped

FOR THE MINT YOGHURT

150 g/5½ fl oz natural yoghurt

15 g/½ oz dried mint

1 teaspoon chilli powder

½ teaspoon salt, or to taste

First make the dough. Blend the yeast with 100 ml/3½ fl oz tepid water. Sift the flours and salt into a large bowl and mix together, then stir in the oil. Make a well in the centre, add the yeast mixture and about 250 ml/9 fl oz water and gradually mix in to make a soft dough.

Knead the dough on a lightly floured surface until smooth and elastic, then put in an oiled bowl, cover with a clean tea towel and leave in a warm place for 15–20 minutes.

Meanwhile, for the filling, finely chop the green parts only of the spring onions, put in a sieve and sprinkle with the salt. Leave to stand for 5 minutes, then gently squeeze the liquid from the onions and transfer to a bowl. Add the remaining filling ingredients and mix well.

Put all the ingredients for the mint yoghurt in a separate bowl and whisk well until smooth. Leave to chill while you make the boulani.

Divide the dough into 12 equal-sized pieces. Roll out each piece on a lightly floured surface into a round about 5 mm/¼ inch thick. Place a spoonful of the filling on one side of each dough round, then spread evenly across one half of the round. Fold the other half over the top of the filling to form a semi-circle. Pinch the open sides together to seal, pat down and sprinkle with a little flour to prevent sticking.

Heat the oil in a large frying pan over a medium heat, add the boulani, in batches, and cook for 2–3 minutes on each side until golden and crisp. Keep the cooked boulani hot while you fry the remainder. Serve with the mint yoghurt.

THE PUNJAB

The land of five rivers. Although the state's economy is agrarian, the migrants to Europe and the US have infused new technologies and ideas into the mainstream of the state. Original Punjabi cuisine was mostly a blend of curries and lentils cooked in clarified butter and rather conservative in its use of spices. Today, however, the cuisine is an amalgamation of spiced curries and rich gravies. The region is famous for tandoori dishes such as tandoori murgh, malai tikka, mutton rara and Amritsari fish. Punjabi food is the most recognised Indian food in Britain today.

Hiren ke Seekh Kebab

Venison kebabs

SERVES 4

500 g/1 lb 2 oz haunch of venison, diced

50 g/1 ³/₄ oz lamb fat, diced

20 g/³/₄ oz Cheddar cheese, grated

2 tablespoons vegetable oil

8 dried figs, chopped

6 cloves garlic, chopped

3 green chillies, chopped

2.5-cm/1-inch piece ginger, peeled and chopped

¹/₂ bunch mint, chopped

¹/₂ bunch coriander, chopped

1 teaspoon garam masala

1 teaspoon chilli powder

1 teaspoon salt, or to taste

sliced red onion, fresh mint leaves and chilli powder, to serve

Put all in the ingredients in a large bowl and mix together well. Pass the mixture through a mincer twice.

Divide the mixture into 8 equal-sized portions. Form each portion into a sausage shape around a metal skewer, then cook in a hot tandoor or over a barbecue for about 5 minutes until cooked through, turning often.

Serve with thinly sliced red onion, fresh mint leaves and a pinch of chilli powder.

Rogani Macchi

Fish curry with onion and yoghurt

SERVES 4

8 sea bass fillets, skinned and pin-boned

FISH MASALA

8 cloves

4 dried red chillies

2 cinnamon sticks

1 teaspoon cumin seeds

1 teaspoon coriander seeds

1/2 teaspoon carom seeds

1/2 teaspoon black peppercorns

FOR THE SAUCE

30 g/1 oz tamarind

2 tomatoes

3 tablespoons vegetable oil

1 teaspoon mustard seeds

1 onion, chopped

2 tablespoons ginger and garlic paste (see page 30)

2 teaspoons ground coriander

1 teaspoon chilli powder

1/2 teaspoon turmeric

1 teaspoon salt, or to taste

2 tablespoons thick natural yoghurt

2 green chillies, slit lengthways

2 red chillies, slit lengthways

few sprigs coriander

2.5-cm/1-inch piece ginger, peeled and cut into julienne

juice of 1 lemon

First prepare the fish masala. Heat a heavy-based frying pan, add all the spices and dry roast over a low heat, shaking the pan frequently, for 5–6 minutes. Leave to cool, then grind in a spice or coffee grinder or with a pestle and mortar to a fine powder.

While the spices are cooling, soak the tamarind in 125 ml/4 fl oz warm water for 20 minutes. Press through a sieve to extract the pulp, discarding the liquid. Blend the tomatoes to a purée in a blender or food processor, then press through a sieve.

Heat the oil in a wok or large frying pan, add the mustard seeds and cook until they crackle. Add the onion and cook until golden brown. Add the ginger and garlic paste, ground coriander, chilli powder, turmeric and salt and cook, stirring, for 2–3 minutes. Whisk the yoghurt with a little water, then add to the pan and cook until the sauce thickens. Add the puréed tomatoes and cook for 8–10 minutes.

Meanwhile, rinse the fish under cold running water, then drain and pat dry with kitchen paper. Cut into chunks.

Add the fish to the sauce and gently simmer for about 10 minutes until cooked. Stir in the chillies, coriander sprigs and ginger julienne and cook for a further minute. Turn off the heat, squeeze over the lemon juice and sprinkle with the fish masala.

LAHORI CHERGHA

Chicken with yoghurt and chillies

SERVES 4

2 whole poussins, each cut
into 4 pieces

10–12 cloves garlic, roughly
chopped

250 g/9 oz thick natural yoghurt

2 teaspoons chilli powder

2 teaspoons ground coriander

I teaspoon turmeric

I teaspoon salt, or to taste

4 tablespoons vegetable oil

12 dried red chillies

I teaspoon cumin seeds

4-cm/I¹/₂-inch piece ginger,
peeled and coarsely grated

few sprigs coriander, chopped

I teaspoon garam masala

10 mixed green and red
chillies, slit lengthways

FOR THE MINT RAITA

¹/₂ teaspoon cumin seeds

¹/₂ teaspoon black peppercorns

200 g/7 oz natural yoghurt

¹/₄ bunch mint leaves

few sprigs coriander

2 cloves garlic, roughly chopped

2 green chillies, roughly chopped

4 tablespoons vegetable oil

¹/₂ teaspoon salt, or to taste

First make the raita. Grind the cumin seeds and peppercorns in a spice or coffee grinder or with a pestle and mortar to a fine powder. Transfer to a blender, add 50 g/I³/₄ oz of the yoghurt and blend to a smooth paste. Add the paste to the remaining yoghurt for the raita in a bowl and whisk together. Add the salt, cover and refrigerate.

Rinse the poussin pieces under cold running water, then drain and pat dry with kitchen paper.

Blend the garlic with 60 g/2¹/₄ oz of the yoghurt in the blender to a smooth paste. Transfer to a large bowl, add the remaining yoghurt, chilli powder, ground coriander, turmeric and salt and mix together well. Add the chicken and turn to coat in the mixture.

Heat the oil in a wok or large frying pan and add the dried red chillies and cumin seeds. When they start to crackle, add the chicken and cook over a high heat for 2–3 minutes until well seared all over. Cover and cook over a low heat, stirring frequently, for about 25 minutes until the chicken is cooked through and tender.

Add the grated ginger, chopped coriander, garam masala and green chillies, stir and cook for I minute. Serve with the mint raita.

KOFTEY

Lamb dumpling curry

SERVES 4

FOR THE KOFTAS

10–12 black peppercorns

6 cloves

1 black cardamom pod

1 cinnamon stick

175 g/6 oz roasted chana
(see page 218)

75 g/2¾ oz poppy seeds

500 g/1 lb 2 oz fatty lamb
mince (5% fat)

1 teaspoon chilli powder

1 teaspoon salt, or to taste

FOR THE SAUCE

40 ml/1½ fl oz vegetable oil

2 onions, sliced

1 tablespoon crushed garlic

1 teaspoon ground coriander

1 teaspoon chilli powder

1 teaspoon turmeric

1 teaspoon salt, or to taste

85 g/3 oz natural yoghurt

1 teaspoon garam masala

few sprigs coriander,
chopped

To make the koftas, grind the peppercorns, cloves, cardamom and cinnamon in a spice or coffee grinder or with a pestle and mortar to a fine powder. Process the roasted chana and poppy seeds in a food processor to a fine powder.

Put the spice powder and chana powder in a large bowl, add the lamb mince, chilli powder and salt and mix well. Transfer to the food processor and process to a paste.

Add 4 tablespoons water to the meat mixture and mix well, then divide the mixture into 12 equal-sized portions and roll each portion into a smooth ball.

Heat the oil for the sauce in a wok or large frying pan, add the onions and cook until golden brown. Add the koftas and cook over a medium heat, stirring frequently, for 3–4 minutes, being careful not to break them up.

Add the garlic paste and cook, stirring, for 2 minutes. Add the coriander, chilli powder, turmeric and salt and cook, stirring, for 1 minute. Add 350 ml/12 fl oz water, cover and cook for 10–15 minutes or until the koftas are tender and the oil separates.

Whisk the yoghurt with 475 ml/17 fl oz water, then add to the pan and cook over a medium heat for 5–6 minutes, stirring frequently. Check the seasoning and cook until the sauce thickens. Sprinkle with the garam masala and scatter over the chopped coriander to finish.

Taka Tak Bheja Masala

Lambs' brains cooked on a griddle

SERVES 4

2 lambs' brains

1/2 teaspoon turmeric

7 cloves garlic, chopped

2 tomatoes, chopped

30 g/1 1/4 oz butter

1 teaspoon chilli powder

1 teaspoon salt, or to taste

1/2 teaspoon crushed black peppercorns

1 teaspoon coriander seeds, crushed

1 tablespoon thick natural yoghurt, whisked

1 teaspoon garam masala

few sprigs coriander chopped

2.5-cm/1-inch piece ginger, peeled and cut into julienne

Cut the lambs' brains into small pieces, rinse under cold running water, then place in a saucepan with enough water to cover. Add the turmeric, bring to the boil and simmer for 5 minutes. Drain.

Heat a large tawa or heavy-based frying pan, add the brains, garlic and tomatoes and then cover and cook for 2–3 minutes or until the tomatoes are tender.

Add the butter and sauté briefly, then add the chilli powder, salt and crushed black peppercorns and coriander seeds and cook, stirring, for 2–3 minutes.

Stir in the yoghurt and cook for a further 5 minutes. Check the seasoning, then sprinkle with the garam masala and scatter with the chopped coriander and ginger julienne before serving.

CHANA KEEMA

Lamb mince stir-fried with chickpeas and seasonal vegetables

SERVES 4

150 g/5½ oz dried chickpeas or 225 g/8 oz drained tinned chickpeas

3 tablespoons vegetable oil

4 black cardamom pods

4 bay leaves

1 teaspoon cumin seeds

1 onion, chopped

2 green chillies, chopped

500 g/1 lb 2 oz coarse lamb mince

1 tablespoon ginger and garlic paste (see page 30)

1 teaspoon chilli powder

½ teaspoon turmeric

2 teaspoons ground coriander

1 teaspoon salt, or to taste

3 tomatoes, chopped

1 teaspoon garam masala

juice of 1 lemon

few sprigs coriander, chopped

ginger julienne, to garnish

If using dried chickpeas, rinse under cold running water and drain, then leave to soak in fresh cold water overnight. Cook in a saucepan of boiling water for about 1½ hours or until tender, topping up the water as necessary.

Meanwhile, heat the oil in a wok or large frying pan. Add the black cardamoms and bay leaves and leave over a gentle heat for a few minutes to allow their flavours to infuse the oil. Add the cumin seeds and cook until they crackle, then add the onion and chillies and cook until the onion is golden brown.

Add the lamb mince and cook over a high heat, breaking up with a wooden spoon, for 5–8 minutes until well browned. Add the ginger and garlic paste and cook, stirring, for 2 minutes. Add the chilli powder, turmeric, ground coriander and salt and cook, stirring, for 1 minute. Stir in the tomatoes and cook for about 6–8 minutes until they are soft.

Add about 400 ml/14 fl oz water to the pan, cover and continue to cook for a further 15 minutes until the lamb is tender. Drain the boiled chickpeas and add to the pan, or simply add the tinned chickpeas, and cook over a low heat for 8–10 minutes. Add the garam masala and check the seasoning.

Turn off the heat, then squeeze in the lemon juice, add the chopped coriander and garnish with ginger julienne.

HALEEM

Lamb with buckwheat and lentils

SERVES 4

125 g/4½ oz bulgur wheat

100 g/3½ oz mixed moong, masoor and chana dal (yellow lentils)

500 g/1 lb 2 oz lean boneless lamb, cut into 2-cm/¾-inch chunks

3 tablespoons vegetable oil

6 cloves

3 cinnamon sticks

6 bay leaves

3 onions, sliced

2 tablespoons ginger and garlic paste (see page 30)

2 teaspoons chilli powder

2 teaspoons ground cumin

1 teaspoon salt

1 teaspoon garam masala

3 tablespoons ghee

few sprigs mint, chopped

few sprigs coriander, chopped

lemon wedges, to serve

Rinse the bulgur wheat under cold running water, then drain and leave to soak in fresh cold water for at least 2 hours. Meanwhile, rinse and drain the lentils and then put in a heavy-based saucepan with double their quantity of water. Bring to the boil, then cook over a medium heat for about 30 minutes until there is no water left and the lentils are thick. Roughly mash the lentils.

Bring a separate saucepan of boiling water to the boil, add the bulgur wheat and stir, then cover and cook over a medium heat for about 20 minutes or according to the packet instructions (bulgur wheat comes in a variety of grain sizes, so cooking times vary).

Rinse the lamb under cold running water, then drain and pat dry with kitchen paper. Heat the oil in a wok or large frying pan and add the cloves, cinnamon sticks and bay leaves. When they start to crackle, add the onions and cook until golden brown. Remove a quarter of the onions with a slotted spoon and drain on kitchen paper.

Add the lamb to the pan and cook over a high heat for 5–8 minutes until well seared all over. Add the ginger and garlic paste and cook, stirring, for 2 minutes. Add the chilli powder, cumin and 1 teaspoon salt or to taste and cook, stirring, for 1 minute. Add enough water to cover the lamb, cover with the lid and cook for 45–50 minutes until the lamb is tender.

Add the boiled lentils and bulgur wheat to the lamb and cook over a medium heat until the mixture has a porridge-like consistency, making sure you keep stirring at all times so that it doesn't stick to the base of the pan. Add the garam masala, ghee and salt to taste.

Turn the heat off, then scatter with the chopped mint and coriander and the reserved fried onions. Serve with lemon wedges.

BHUNI SHAKARKANDI

Roasted sweet potato

SERVES 4

4 sweet potatoes

1 teaspoon chilli powder

1 teaspoon ground cumin

1 teaspoon amchoor
(dried mango powder)

1 teaspoon salt, or to taste

juice of 1 lemon

1 red chilli, roughly sliced

few sprigs coriander, torn

2.5-cm/1-inch piece ginger,
peeled and roughly chopped

Preheat the oven to 180°C/350°F/gas 4. Wrap the sweet potatoes in foil and bake them in the oven for about 35 minutes or until tender. Leave until cool enough to handle, then peel and cut into 2.5-cm/1-inch rounds.

Put the sweet potato in a bowl, add the chilli powder, cumin, amchoor and salt and mix well. Squeeze over the lemon juice, then add the chilli, coriander and ginger. Serve warm.

Luqmiyan

Mini lamb samosas

SERVES 4

FOR THE PASTRY

225 g/8 oz plain flour,
plus extra for rolling out
and sealing

pinch salt, or to taste

2 tablespoons vegetable oil,
plus extra for rolling out
and deep-frying

Tamarind chutney
(see page 133), to serve

FOR THE FILLING

125 g/4 oz dried green peas

5-cm/2-inch piece ginger,
peeled and roughly chopped

8 cloves garlic, roughly
chopped

3 tablespoons vegetable oil

1 teaspoon cumin seeds

1 onion, chopped

500 g/1 lb 2 oz lamb mince

1½ teaspoons crushed dried
red chillies

1 teaspoon ground coriander

½ teaspoon turmeric

1 teaspoon salt, or to taste

1 tablespoon amchoor
(dried mango powder)

few sprigs coriander, chopped

juice of 1 lemon

For the filling, rinse the dried peas under cold running water, then drain and leave to soak in fresh cold water for 3 hours.

Drain the peas and cook in a saucepan of boiling water for 20–25 minutes until tender but still whole, then drain.

Meanwhile, make the pastry. Sift the flour and salt into a large bowl and mix together, then stir in the oil. Make a well in the centre, add 120 ml/4 fl oz water and gradually mix in to make a firm dough. Cover with a clean damp tea towel and leave to rest for 30 minutes.

Pound the ginger and garlic together in a pestle and mortar until crushed. Heat the oil in a wok or large frying pan, add the cumin seeds and cook until they crackle. Add the crushed ginger and garlic and sauté, stirring, for 2 minutes. Add the onion and cook until soft and translucent. Add the lamb mince and cook over a medium heat, breaking up with a wooden spoon, for 8–9 minutes until browned. Add the crushed chillies, ground coriander, turmeric and salt and stir well. Stir in the boiled peas and sauté for 2 minutes. Turn off the heat and leave to cool, then stir in the amchoor, chopped coriander and lemon juice. Check the seasoning.

Divide the pastry dough into 6 equal-sized pieces. Roll out each piece of dough on a lightly floured surface into a 25 cm/10-inch round. Take one round and sprinkle with a few drops of oil, then cover with a layer of flour. Place a second round on top and roll out very thinly, using a little flour if necessary to prevent sticking.

Heat a tawa or a non-stick frying pan, add the stacked pastry rounds (roti) and cook for 20 seconds on each side. Remove and separate the roti. Leave to cool, then cut each roti into quarters. Keep the roti covered with a clean damp tea towel to prevent them drying out. Repeat the process with the remaining dough.

Mix 1 tablespoon flour with 1 tablespoon water to make a smooth paste. Take one roti quarter, brush the straight edges with the flour paste and form into a cone shape around your fingers, sealing the edges. Spoon a tablespoonful of the filling mixture into the cone, brush the rounded edge with flour paste and fold over to enclose the filling and form a triangle, making sure that you seal the parcel well. Repeat with the remaining roti quarters.

Heat enough oil for deep-frying in a wok or deep saucepan to 180–190°C/350°–375°F, or until a cube of bread browns in 30 seconds. Add the parcels, one at a time, and deep-fry until golden brown and crisp. Remove and drain on kitchen paper. Keep hot while cooking the remaining parcels. Serve with Tamarind chutney.

Mash Ki Dal

White lentils with spices

SERVES 4

300 g/10½ oz urad dal
(white lentils)

1 tablespoon crushed dried
red chillies

1 tablespoon ground
coriander

1 teaspoon turmeric

1 teaspoon salt, or to taste

5-cm/2-inch piece ginger,
peeled and roughly chopped

7 cloves garlic, peeled and
roughly chopped

3 tablespoons vegetable oil

1 tablespoon cumin seeds

1 onion, sliced

6 green chillies, chopped

few sprigs coriander,
chopped, to garnish

Rinse the lentils under cold running water, then drain. Leave to soak in fresh cold water for at least 2 hours, then drain.

Put the lentils in a heavy-based saucepan with double their quantity of water, the crushed chillies, ground coriander, turmeric and salt. Bring to the boil, then cook over a medium heat for about 20 minutes until there is no water left and the lentils are just tender but still whole.

Meanwhile, crush the ginger and garlic together with a pestle and mortar. Heat the oil in a wok or large frying pan, add the cumin seeds and cook until they crackle. Add the crushed ginger and garlic, onion and green chillies and cook until the onion is golden brown.

Add the onion mixture to the cooked lentils and stir it in only slightly. Check the seasoning and garnish with the chopped coriander.

ALOO METHI KA SAAG

Potatoes with fenugreek

SERVES 4

4 bunches fresh fenugreek

50 ml/2 fl oz vegetable oil

1 teaspoon cumin seeds

2.5-cm/1-inch piece ginger, peeled and roughly chopped

2 green chillies, slit lengthways

1 teaspoon ground coriander

½ teaspoon chilli powder

¼ teaspoon turmeric

1 teaspoon salt, or to taste

8 baby new potatoes, washed and sliced

2–3 teaspoons puréed fresh tomato (optional)

juice of 1 lemon

½ teaspoon garam masala

few sprigs coriander, chopped

Discard the stems of the fenugreek and chop the leaves. Rinse under cold running water, then drain and pat dry with kitchen paper.

Heat half the oil in a wok or large frying pan, add half the cumin seeds and cook until they crackle, then add the fenugreek and cook over a low heat until the leaves have wilted. Remove from the pan and set aside.

Heat the remaining oil in the pan, add the remaining cumin seeds and cook until they crackle. Add the ginger and chillies and sauté, stirring, for 1 minute, then add the ground coriander, chilli powder, turmeric and salt and sauté, stirring, for 2 minutes.

Add potatoes and cook over a low heat until almost tender, then add the fenugreek and the tomato purée, if you like, and cook over a medium heat for 3–4 minutes. Check the seasoning, then squeeze over the lemon juice, sprinkle with the garam masala and scatter with the chopped coriander.

THE ROAD TO THE PUNJAB

LEAVING DELHI EARLY IN THE MORNING. A duvet of fog nestles gently upon the still sleeping city. I'm heading west to Punjab proper and the town of Ambala. The fog around Delhi has been exacerbated by pollution in recent years but in truth it has always been an issue. Delhi is surrounded by arid, dry lands. New Delhi is a 'constructed' city; the modern incarnation of an ancient culture. The creation of one of this city has irrevocably changed the microclimatic balance of the region.

Travelling down the GT road we are heading for Puran Singh ka Dhaba, probably one of the best places for Punjabi food on the road. It's 200 km away, about a four-hour drive. Before I left London Ani was evangelical that if all else fails, if the rivers burst their banks, the trees are set alight by lightening and the grey, foreboding sky falls in, I must still, somehow, by hook or by crook, make my way to a dhaba across the road from the bus station in Ambala. Forgiving Ani his hyperbole, I promised that Puran Singh ka Dhaba would be visited.

On the road out of the easterly suburbs of the capital we pass Azadpur Mundi, the wholesale fruit and vegetable market, a cornucopia of deliciousness. There isn't a country in the world that displays fruit and veg the way Indians do… there's art, geometry, pride and love; it's a delight to behold fruit and vegetables for sale on the sub-continent. The name of the market is a statement of history. Azadpur means land of the free. On the other side of the mundi is a neighbourhood called Jahangir Puri.

After partition Hindus and Sikhs left their homes, their lives and their histories in the newly created Pakistan; they travelled south down the GT Road into post-August 1947 India. They arrived, dazed and confused, in the outskirts of Delhi where they were given land to settle.

It was called Jang Pura, the place of the fighters. During the autumn of 1947 what was once agricultural land became a ghetto. People arrived with nothing but the clothes on their backs, the immediate pain of change and long, often unforgiving memories. They were each given a plot of land and a tarpaulin. Forty or so years later Jahangit Puri was one of the most vibrant and entrepreneurial neighbourhoods in Delhi. By the 1980s the residents had made their money and moved out. And life moved on a click. Quite a transition, and all on the GT Road.

I stop at Sukhdev ka Dhaba for a breakfast of parathas and dhai; paneer and anda and boondi ka dhai. And of course chai. The place is massive, maybe space for 400 diners. It's like a B&Q-style dhaba in terms of sheer scale. I'm surrounded by Punjabis. Wherever I look there's a gaily coloured turban and a woman in a shawl. I am the only man in a gaily coloured turban also wearing a shawl; it is clear I'm almost home.

I'm effervescing with excitement at the very thought of Puran Singh ka Dhaba. It sounds like a unique place. That is until you find out that there are now any number of Puran Singh ka Dhabas in and around Ambala. This one, the original, is near the bus station. There's a story, apocryphal perhaps, that all the other dhaba owners pay Puran Singh ka Dhaba to close after lunch, thereby allowing them a little custom. The free market never fails to surprise me.

The original Puran Singh set up shop on the GT Road in 1955, selling from a simple hand-cart on the edge of the road. He sold three curries: mutton, chicken and keema (mince). As his reputation grew so did his business and he opened a small stall on the opposite side of the road a couple of years later. He retired and gave his business to his meat supplier in the 1990s. He expanded the site to almost 200 covers. As I sit and eat an amazing mince curry embellished with chunks of liver, I can see exactly where Puran Singh started with his cart, some fifty yards away. Ironic that a few hundred yards away on the GT Road is a massive billboard for Nandos. I know where I would rather be.

Farmlands stretch out on either side, as far as the eye can see. Green and brown vistas punctuated by the occasional pink-turbanned tractor driver. The GT road is arterial, crucial to the economy of the Punjab. Punjab is and has been the agriculture heart of India. It is one of the most fertile regions on the planet. This is reflected in the very name of the area. Punjab mean 'five rivers' and to this day the five rivers of the Punjab are an integral part of the topography and society of the state. It is this very fact that has kept the soil irrigated. The Himalayan topsoil, the most minerally rich soil in the world, has drifted the few hundred kilometres down those rivers to these lands. With the flow of fecundity came the flow of prosperity.

Modern-day Punjab is a shadow of its magnificent former self. The kingdom once governed by Maharajah Ranjit Singh has in the last two hundred years dwindled to almost nothing. Partition saw more than half of Punjab, and our historic capital city Lahore, gifted to Pakistan. The remaining Indian Punjab was whittled into three new states: Haryana, Himachel Pradesh and modern Punjab. Being Punjabi and being a Sikh can be a frustrating experience when one remembers how great a history, how grand an Empire we once controlled. All the way to Kabul.

The changes haven't been purely political. Over-farming, pesticide, fertilisers and new damming procedures have now killed the land of the Punjab. The halcyon days are over. Less than 5% of the fields of the Punjab are tilled in the traditional way. The rest have embraced the 'green revolution' and genetic modification. They call it progress...

Progressing from Ambala to Amritsar is no mean feat. Nearly five hours on the GT. The closer you get to Amritsar the more prolific the dhabas appear until at one point, 20 km shy of the Spiritual Home of the Sikhs, they appear in clutches of seven or eight.

Amritsar is a special place. I'm afraid I can be anything but objective about the place. I have family that live there, ancestors that came from there and my own vivid memories of the city. I first came here when I was seven and have loved it ever since.

The city is pretty clean, well-laid out and organised. Its central focus is the Golden Temple, the holiest shrine of the Sikhs. I've travelled over 3000 kilometres and have yet to eat tandoori anything. Where better to break that fast than in Amritsar? Punjabis are to tandoori what Heston is to innovation. And snails.

Bubby's Dhaba on Lawrence Rd, a busy corner in the heart of Amritsar. Out front I watch a massive handi full of onions boil and bubble without toil or trouble. Another man makes fresh tandoori naans; a third man adds tarka to dal. Inside is smaller than a cheap flat in Soho: space for 20 normal folk or 17 big-shouldered (and equally big-turbanned) Sikhs. A TV spouts uselessness from its wall mounting. This is one of the few times in my eating life (outside of a family gathering) where the men in turbans are the overwhelming majority. It feels good.

Tandoori chicken, mutton tikka, dal makhani. Pure Punjabi food in pure Punjabi country... a hop, skip and a thump from the GT road.

This is the best tandoori chicken I have ever tasted. It was clean, subtly spiced, straight out of the oven some five yards from where I was sitting. The chicken itself tasted of chicken, tender and soft. There's none of the radioactive Chernobyl-red tandoori style chicken that greets you on every high street the length and breadth of the UK. This is a symphony of soft orange-spiced chicken, enveloped harmoniously in a hot buttered naan: it was perfect. The dal makhani combined ma di dal (black lentil) with the rajmah (kidney bean). And of course enough butter to last a Hampshire family of four for a week and a half. The mutton tikka was darkly intense, almost satanic in its flavourings. Without doubt, Bubby's chicken was one of the stars of GT Road and the perfect place to end my journey. For now...

191

SARSON KA SAAG

Creamed mustard leaves

SERVES 4

500 g/1 lb 2 oz green
mustard leaves

250 g/9 oz spinach leaves

2 green chillies, chopped

1 teaspoon salt, or to taste

3 tablespoons vegetable oil

1 teaspoon cumin seeds

5 cloves garlic, crushed

1 onion, chopped

3 tomatoes, chopped

½ tablespoon chilli powder

50 g/1¾ oz maize flour

1 teaspoon garam masala

juice of 1 lemon

butter, to serve

Discard the stems of both the greens. Rinse thoroughly under cold running water, then drain lightly.

Put the greens in a large saucepan with just the water left clinging to the leaves and add the chillies and salt. Cover and bring to the boil. Drain and leave to cool, then blend in a blender or food processor to a coarse paste.

Heat the oil in a wok or large frying pan, add the cumin seeds and cook until they crackle. Add the garlic and cook, stirring, for 2 minutes. Add the onion and cook until soft and translucent. Stir in the tomatoes and chilli powder and cook for about 15 minutes until the tomatoes are tender.

Add the flour and cook, stirring frequently, for 3–4 minutes, then add the blended greens and cook, stirring, for 6–7 minutes. Turn off the heat, sprinkle with the garam masala and squeeze over the lemon juice. Check the seasoning, then serve topped with a small knob of butter.

ALOO WADI HARA PYAZ

Lentil dumplings with potatoes and spring onion

SERVES 4

vegetable oil, for deep-frying
and sautéing

4–5 Punjabi wadi (lentil
dumplings)

2.5-cm/1-inch piece ginger,
peeled and roughly chopped

6 cloves garlic, roughly chopped

few sprigs coriander, roughly
chopped

3 green chillies, roughly chopped

1/2 teaspoon mustard seeds

1/2 teaspoon cumin seeds

4 dried red chillies

2 onions, chopped

1/2 teaspoon chilli powder

1/4 teaspoon turmeric

I teaspoon salt, or to taste

2 tomatoes, chopped

6 potatoes, peeled and diced

I bunch spring onions, chopped

1/2 teaspoon masala powder
(see below)

juice of I lemon

FOR THE MASALA POWDER

I teaspoon cumin seeds

I teaspoon coriander seeds

1/2 teaspoon fennel seeds

1/4 teaspoon black peppercorns

1/4 teaspoon ground ginger

First prepare the masala powder. Heat a heavy-based frying pan, add all the spices except the ground ginger and dry roast over a low heat, shaking the pan frequently, for 5–6 minutes. Leave to cool, then grind with the ground ginger in a spice or coffee grinder or with a pestle and mortar to a fine powder.

Heat enough oil for deep-frying in a wok or deep saucepan to 180–190°C/350°–375°F, or until a cube of bread browns in 30 seconds. Add the wadi and deep-fry in batches until golden brown. Remove and drain on kitchen paper. Transfer to a bowl of hot water and leave to soak for 2–3 minutes, then drain.

Blend the ginger, garlic, coriander and green chillies in a blender with enough water to make a smooth paste.

Heat 2 tablespoons oil in the wok or a large frying pan, add the mustard and cumin seeds and dried red chillies and cook until they crackle, then add the onion and cook until soft and translucent. Stir in the ginger paste and cook, stirring frequently, for 3–4 minutes.

Add the chilli powder, turmeric and salt to taste, and mix well, then add the tomatoes, cover and cook until tender. Add the diced potatoes and cook for 2 minutes, then stir in about 125 ml/4 fl oz water, cover and cook for 10–12 minutes until the potatoes are tender.

Add the wadi and spring onions and cook, stirring, for a minute or so, then add a little water to make sure there is enough sauce and bring to the boil. Turn off the heat and finish by sprinkling with the masala powder and squeezing over the lemon juice.

RARHA GOSHT

Lamb curry

1 kg/2 lb 4 oz lamb cutlets, on the bone

300 g/10½ oz lamb mince

40 ml/1½ fl oz vegetable oil

2 bay leaves

3 black cardamom pods

4 green cardamom pods

1 cinnamon stick

3 onions, chopped

3 tablespoons ginger and garlic paste (see page 30)

1 tablespoon ground coriander

1 teaspoon turmeric

1 teaspoon chilli powder

1 teaspoon salt, or to taste

2 tomatoes, chopped

125 g/4 oz thick natural yoghurt

1 teaspoon garam masala

juice of 1 lemon

few sprigs coriander, chopped

Rinse the cutlets and mince separately under cold running water, then drain and pat dry with kitchen paper.

Heat the oil in a large frying pan, add the bay leaves, black and green cardamoms and cinnamon stick and leave for a few minutes over a gentle heat to allow their flavours to infuse the oil. Add the onions and cook until golden brown.

Add the cutlets and cook over a high heat for 2 minutes on each side until well seared. Stir in the ginger and garlic paste and cook, stirring, for 2 minutes. Add the ground coriander, turmeric, chilli powder and salt and mix well, then add the tomatoes and cook for about 15 minutes until tender.

Whisk the yoghurt with enough cold water to make a pouring consistency, then add to the curry, cover and cook for about 15 minutes. Stir in the lamb mince and cook for 10–12 minutes until the mince is fully cooked and the cutlets are tender.

Turn off the heat, then sprinkle with the garam masala, squeeze over the lemon juice and scatter with the chopped coriander before serving.

GURDEY

Lambs' kidney masala

SERVES 4

1 kg/2 lb 4 oz lambs' kidneys

2 tablespoons vegetable oil

2 onions, sliced

1 tablespoon ginger and
garlic paste (see page 30)

1 teaspoon turmeric

1 teaspoon chilli powder

1 teaspoon crushed dried
red chillies

1 teaspoon salt, or to taste

2 tomatoes, chopped

1 teaspoon ground cumin

1 teaspoon dried fenugreek
leaves, crumbled

½ teaspoon garam masala

few sprigs coriander,
chopped

2 green chillies, slit
lengthways

2.5-cm/1-inch piece ginger,
peeled and cut into julienne

juice of 1 lemon

butter, to serve (optional)

Rinse the kidneys under cold running water, then drain and pat dry with kitchen paper. Put in a saucepan, cover with cold water and bring to the boil, then drain.

Heat the oil in a wok or large frying pan, add the onions and cook until golden brown. Add the ginger and garlic paste and cook, stirring, for 2 minutes, then add the turmeric, chilli powder, crushed chillies and salt and mix well.

Add the boiled kidneys and cook over a high heat until well seared all over. Add the tomatoes, cover and cook for about 15 minutes until tender. Stir in the cumin and fenugreek, cover and cook for a further 5 minutes.

Turn off the heat, then sprinkle with the garam masala, scatter with the chopped coriander, green chillies and ginger julienne and squeeze over the lemon juice. For a traditional finishing touch, serve with a small knob of butter on top.

TEETARI

Tandoor roasted guinea fowl

SERVES 4

12 dried Kashmiri red
chillies

1 whole guinea fowl, skinned
and cut into 8 pieces

4 tablespoons malt vinegar

1½ teaspoons chilli powder

1 teaspoon salt

4-cm/1½-inch piece ginger,
peeled and roughly chopped

10 cloves garlic, roughly
chopped

40 ml/1½ fl oz mustard oil

90 g/3¼ oz hung yoghurt
(see page 219)

½ teaspoon caraway seeds

1 teaspoon garam masala

chutneys, to serve

Discard the stems of the chillies, slit open and discard the seeds. Put in a heatproof bowl, cover with boiling water and leave to soak for 1 hour, then drain.

Rinse the guinea fowl pieces under cold running water, then drain and pat dry with kitchen paper. Make incisions in the breasts and legs with a sharp knife.

Mix together the vinegar, chilli powder and 1 teaspoon salt in a large non-metallic bowl. Add the guinea fowl pieces and mix well, then cover and leave to marinate for about 15–20 minutes at cool room temperature.

Meanwhile, put the ginger, garlic, mustard oil and soaked Kashmiri chillies in a blender and blend to a smooth paste. Transfer to shallow dish, add the yoghurt, caraway seeds and salt to taste and mix well. Add the guinea fowl pieces and turn to coat in the mixture, then cover and leave to marinate in the fridge for 3–4 hours.

Thread the guinea fowl pieces onto metal skewers and cook in a medium-high tandoor or over a barbecue for about 15 minutes or until cooked through. Allow to rest for a couple of minutes before sprinkling with garam masala and serving.

Suvey aur Palak ka Gosht

Lamb masala with whole spices

SERVES 4

1 kg/2 lb 4 oz boneless leg of lamb, cut into 2.5-cm/ 1-inch chunks

40 ml/1½ fl oz vegetable oil

2 green cardamom pods

1 cinnamon stick

2 black cardamom pods

2 bay leaves

3–4 cloves

2 onions, chopped

4 tomatoes

2 tablespoons ginger and garlic paste (see page 30)

2 teaspoons ground coriander

2 teaspoons chilli powder

½ teaspoon turmeric

1 teaspoon salt

85 g/3 oz thick natural yoghurt

handful baby spinach leaves

few sprigs dill, chopped

2.5-cm/1-inch piece ginger, peeled and cut into julienne

juice of 1 lemon

1 teaspoon garam masala

½ teaspoon ground black cardamom

Rinse the lamb under cold running water, then drain and pat dry with kitchen paper.

Heat the oil in a large frying pan, add the whole spices and cook until they crackle, then add the onions and cook until golden brown.

Meanwhile, blend the tomatoes in a blender or food processor to a smooth purée.

Add the lamb to the pan and cook over a high heat until well seared all over. Stir in the ginger and garlic paste and cook, stirring, for 2 minutes. Add the coriander, chilli powder, turmeric and salt and cook, stirring frequently, for 2–3 minutes.

Stir in the puréed tomatoes and yoghurt and cook for about 15 minutes until the oil separates, then add enough water to the pan to cover the lamb, cover with a lid and simmer gently for about 1 hour or until the lamb is tender. Stir in the spinach, dill and ginger julienne and cook for a further 2 minutes.

Turn off the heat, then squeeze over the lemon juice, sprinkle with the garam masala and black cardamom and check the seasoning before serving.

KADHI PAKORA

Chickpea flour dumplings in yoghurt

SERVES 4

FOR THE PAKORAS
200 g/7 oz chickpea flour
1 teaspoon carom seeds
1 teaspoon chilli powder
½ teaspoon turmeric
¼ teaspoon baking powder
2 green chillies, chopped
4-cm/1½-inch piece ginger, peeled and chopped
3 onions, chopped
2 handfuls spinach leaves, chopped
1 teaspoon salt, or to taste
vegetable oil, for deep-frying

FOR THE KADHI
100 g/3½ oz chickpea flour
200 g/7 oz thick natural yoghurt
1 teaspoon chilli powder
½ teaspoon turmeric
1 teaspoon salt, or to taste
3 tablespoons vegetable oil
½ teaspoon cumin seeds
½ teaspoon mustard seeds
2 dried red chillies
7 cloves garlic, chopped
pinch ground asafoetida
1 onion, chopped
juice of 1 lemon
few sprigs coriander, chopped, to garnish

First make the pakoras. Put all the pakora ingredients except the oil in a large bowl and mix together thoroughly. Make a well in the centre, add about 5–6 tablespoons of water and gradually mix in to make a thick batter. Add a little more water if necessary. Beat together thoroughly.

Heat enough oil for deep-frying in an Indian wok or deep saucepan to 180–190°C/350°–375°F, or until a cube of bread browns in 30 seconds. Add tablespoonfuls of the pakora mixture and deep-fry until crisp and golden brown. Remove with a slotted spoon and leave to drain on kitchen paper.

For the kadhi, mix together the chickpea flour, yoghurt, chilli powder, turmeric and salt in a bowl. Whisk in 500 ml/18 fl oz water until smooth. Transfer to the mixture to a heavy-based saucepan and cook over a medium heat, stirring frequently, for 10–15 minutes until it comes to the boil. Turn the heat to low and leave to simmer.

Heat the oil in a wok or large frying pan, add the whole spices, dried chillies, garlic and asafoetida and cook until they crackle, then add the onion and cook until golden brown. Add to the kadhi mixture and cook for 5–6 minutes.

Turn off the heat and add the fried pakoras. Squeeze over the lemon juice and check the seasoning, then scatter with the chopped coriander to garnish.

Paneer Bhurji

Scrambled paneer with spices

SERVES 4

FOR THE PANEER

1 litre/1¾ pints full-fat milk

200 ml/ 7 fl oz double cream

2 tablespoons white vinegar

½ teaspoon ground cumin

few sprigs coriander, chopped

FOR THE SAUCE

2 tablespoons vegetable oil

1 teaspoon cumin seeds

2.5-cm/1-inch piece ginger, peeled and chopped

2 green chillies, chopped

1 onion, chopped

1 teaspoon chilli powder

1 teaspoon ground coriander

¼ teaspoon turmeric

1 teaspoon salt, or to taste

2 tomatoes, chopped

1 green pepper, deseeded and chopped

1 yellow pepper, deseeded and chopped

1 red pepper, deseeded chopped

juice of 1 lemon

½ teaspoon garam masala

few sprigs coriander, chopped

First make the paneer. Put the milk and cream in a saucepan and bring to the boil, then add the vinegar, cumin and chopped coriander, stirring the milk mixture slowly. Continue stirring over a high heat until the whey separates, then pour the mixture into a piece of muslin, tie loosely at the top with string and hang over a bowl until the liquid drains off.

Place a heavy weight over the paneer in the muslin for at least 30 minutes and leave until completely cool. Grate the paneer, cover and set aside.

To make the sauce, heat the oil in a large frying pan, add the cumin seeds and cook until they crackle, then add the ginger and chillies and sauté for 1 minute. Add the onion and cook until golden brown, then add the chilli powder, ground coriander, turmeric and salt and cook, stirring, for 2 minutes. Add the tomatoes and cook for about 15 minutes, then stir in the peppers and cook for 2–3 minutes.

Add the grated paneer to the pan and cook, stirring, for 2 minutes. Turn off the heat, then squeeze over the lemon juice, sprinkle with the garam masala and scatter with the chopped coriander.

Ambarsari Macchi

Fried fish with spices

SERVES 4

4 fish steaks

juice of 1 lemon

4-cm/1½-inch piece ginger, peeled and chopped

2 green chillies, chopped

2 tablespoons ginger and garlic paste (see page 30)

1 tablespoon chilli powder

1 teaspoon carom seeds

1 teaspoon salt, or to taste

125 g/4 oz chickpea flour

40 g/1½ oz rice flour

few sprigs coriander, chopped

vegetable oil, for deep-frying

1 teaspoon amchoor (dried mango powder)

TO SERVE

Mint and coriander chutney (see page 133)

lemon wedges

Rinse the fish under cold running water, then drain and pat dry with kitchen paper.

Mix together the lemon juice, ginger, chillies, ginger and garlic paste, chilli powder, carom seeds and salt in a shallow non-metallic dish. Add the fish steaks and turn to coat in the mixture, then cover and leave to marinate at cool room temperature for 20 minutes.

Add the flours and chopped coriander to the marinated fish and sprinkle over about 2 tablespoons of water so that the flour mixture lightly coats the fish.

Heat enough oil for deep-frying in a wok or deep saucepan to 180–190°C/350°–375°F, or until a cube of bread browns in 30 seconds. Deep-fry the fish steaks, in 2 batches, until crisp and golden brown. Remove and drain on kitchen paper. Keep the cooked fish hot while cooking the remainder.

Sprinkle the fish with the amchoor and serve with Mint and coriander chutney and lemon wedges for squeezing over.

Kararee Bhyein

Lotus stems tossed with peanut and coriander

SERVES 4

600 g/1 lb 5 oz lotus stems

vegetable oil, for deep-frying

70 g/2½ oz raw unsalted peanuts, skinned

1 teaspoon chilli powder

1 tablespoon amchoor (dried mango powder)

1 teaspoon roasted ground cumin

5-cm/2-inch piece ginger, peeled and cut into julienne

1 teaspoon salt, or to taste

juice of 1 lemon

few sprigs coriander, chopped

Peel the lotus stems, then thinly slice, preferably with a mandolin. Rinse under cold running water, then drain well and pat dry with kitchen paper.

Heat enough oil for deep-frying in a wok or deep saucepan to 180–190°C/350°–375°F, or until a cube of bread browns in 30 seconds. Add the lotus stem slices and deep-fry until crisp. Remove and drain on kitchen paper.

Heat a heavy-based frying pan and dry roast the peanuts, shaking the pan frequently, until golden brown. Leave to cool, then crush in a food processor or put in a double layer of plastic bags and bash with a rolling pin.

Put the chilli powder, amchoor, roasted ground cumin, roasted peanuts, fried lotus stems, ginger and salt in a large bowl. Squeeze over the lemon juice and mix together lightly, taking care not to crush the lotus stems. Sprinkle with the chopped coriander.

MUTTER PARANTHA

Bread stuffed with green peas

SERVES 4

450 g/1 lb wholewheat flour, plus extra for dusting

pinch salt, or to taste

2 tablespoons vegetable oil

FOR THE FILLING

250 g/9 oz peas, defrosted if frozen

about 150 ml/5½ fl oz vegetable oil

½ teaspoon cumin seeds

2.5-cm/1-inch piece ginger, peeled and chopped

2 green chillies, chopped

¼ teaspoon ground asafoetida

½ teaspoon chilli powder

1 teaspoon salt, or to taste

½ teaspoon garam masala

juice of 1 lemon

few sprigs coriander, chopped

1 teaspoon amchoor (dried mango powder)

TO SERVE

natural yoghurt

Cauliflower and turnip pickle (see page 134)

First make the filling. Cook the peas in a saucepan of boiling water for 5–7 minutes until tender. Drain and leave to cool, then mash.

Heat 2 tablespoons of the oil in a wok or large frying pan, add the cumin seeds and cook until they crackle. Add the ginger, chillies and asafoetida and cook, stirring, for 30 seconds. Add the mashed peas, chilli powder and salt, mix well and cook for 5 minutes. Stir in the garam masala and lemon juice, then transfer the mixture to a bowl and leave to cool completely. Once cold, stir in the chopped coriander and amchoor.

Meanwhile, to make the parantha, sift the flour and salt into a large bowl and mix together, then stir in the oil. Make a well in the centre, add about 120 ml/7 fl oz water and gradually mix in to make a soft dough. Cover with a clean damp tea towel and leave to stand for 30 minutes.

Divide the dough into 6 equal-sized pieces, then roll out each piece of dough on a lightly floured surface into an 8-cm/3-inch round. Divide the filling between the dough rounds, spooning it into the centre, then fold in the edges and gently roll each piece into a smooth ball, making sure that the filing doesn't ooze out.

Flatten the stuffed parantha and roll again, this time into circles about 15 cm/6 inches in diameter. Dust with a little flour if required to prevent sticking.

Heat a large tawa or non-stick frying pan. Brush one side of a parantha with 1 teaspoon of the remaining oil, then add to the pan, oil side down, and cook over a medium heat until golden and crisp. Brush the top with another teaspoon of the oil, turn over and cook the second side until golden and crisp. Remove from the pan and keep hot while cooking the remaining parantha in the same way.

Serve the parantha with yogurt and Cauliflower and turnip pickle.

Jungli Soor ka Achar

Spicy wild boar pickle

SERVES 4

500 g/1 lb 2 oz wild boar
steak, cut into 2.5-cm/1-inch
chunks

vegetable oil, for deep-frying
and sautéing

1 teaspoon mustard seeds

2.5-cm/1-inch piece ginger,
peeled and chopped

7 cloves garlic, chopped

3 green chillies, chopped

2 tablespoons red chilli paste
(see page 212)

1 tablespoon masala
(see below)

1 teaspoon salt, or to taste

50 ml/2 fl oz white vinegar

FOR THE MASALA

4 tablespoons fennel seeds

2 tablespoons coriander seeds

2 tablespoons cumin seeds

1 teaspoon fenugreek seeds

Rinse the wild boar chunks under cold running water, then drain and pat dry with kitchen paper.

Heat enough oil for deep-frying in a wok or deep saucepan to 180–190°C/350°–375°F, or until a cube of bread browns in 30 seconds. Deep-fry the wild boar chunks, in batches, until crisp and golden brown. Remove with a slotted spoon, drain on kitchen paper and leave to cool.

Heat 150 ml/5½ fl oz vegetable oil in a large, heavy-based frying pan, add the mustard seeds and cook until they crackle, then add the ginger, garlic and chillies and cook, stirring frequently, until golden brown.

Meanwhile, grind the spices for the masala together in a spice or coffee grinder or with a pestle and mortar to a fine powder. Store in an airtight container.

Add the chilli paste to the pan and cook until the oil separates, then add the masala and salt and mix well. Add the vinegar and fried wild boar and cook for 7–8 minutes. Check the seasoning, then turn off the heat and leave to cool. Store in an airtight container in the fridge for 2 days before eating. It will keep up to 1 week, but make sure there is enough oil to cover the pickle at all times, as the oil acts as a preservative; top up if necessary.

Andey Ka Achar

Quails' egg pickle

SERVES 4

2 dozen quails' eggs

vegetable oil, for deep-frying

3 teaspoons ground coriander

2 teaspoons chilli powder

1 teaspoon turmeric

150 ml/5½ fl oz mustard oil

1 teaspoon whole panch phoran (see below)

2.5-cm/1-inch piece ginger, peeled and chopped

3 green chillies, chopped

1 tablespoon ground panch phoran (see below)

1 teaspoon salt, or to taste

juice of 3 lemons

FOR THE PANCH PHORAN

2 tablespoons fennel seeds

2 tablespoons black mustard seeds

2 tablespoons cumin seeds

2 tablespoons nigella seeds

1 teaspoon fenugreek seeds

First make the panch phoran. Mix all the spices together in a bowl, then store in an airtight container in a cool, dry, dark place and use as required.

To make the pickle, cook the quails' eggs in a saucepan of boiling water for 3 minutes until hard-boiled. Drain, leave to cool, then peel.

Heat enough vegetable oil for deep-frying in a wok or deep saucepan to 180–190°C/350°–375°F, or until a cube of bread browns in 30 seconds. Deep-fry the quails' eggs, in batches, until golden brown. Remove with a slotted spoon and drain on kitchen paper, then transfer to a bowl. Mix together half the coriander, chilli powder and turmeric, sprinkle over the eggs and toss to coat.

Heat the mustard oil in a large, heavy-based frying pan, add the whole panch phoran and cook until the spices crackle, then add the ginger and chillies and cook, stirring, for 2 minutes. Stir in the remaining coriander, chilli powder and turmeric with the ground panch phoran and salt and cook for 1 minute. Add the lemon juice and mix well.

Turn off the heat, add the fried quails' eggs to the pan and mix together. Check the seasoning, then leave to cool. Store in an airtight container in the fridge for up to a week. This is best made 2 days before you want to eat it.

TEETAR KA ACHAR

Partridge pickle

SERVES 4

12 dried red chillies

2 partridges with skin, boned
(ask your butcher to do this)

200 ml/7 fl oz mustard oil

2 tablespoons ginger and
garlic paste (see page 30)

2 teaspoons chilli powder

1 teaspoon salt, or to taste

2 teaspoons mustard seeds

few curry leaves

5-cm/2-inch piece ginger,
peeled and chopped

10 cloves garlic, chopped

2 green chillies, chopped

2 tablespoons ground
coriander

1/4 teaspoon ground asafoetida

100 ml/3½ fl oz white vinegar

To make red chilli paste, discard the dried chilli stems, put in a heatproof bowl and cover with boiling water. Leave to soak for 1 hour, then drain and blend in a blender to a paste, adding a little water if necessary.

Cut each partridge into large chunks. Rinse under cold running water, then drain and pat dry with kitchen paper.

Mix together 50 ml/2 fl oz of the oil, 1 tablespoon of the ginger and garlic paste, 1 teaspoon of the chilli powder and salt in a bowl. Add the partridge pieces and turn to coat in the oil mixture, then cover and leave to marinate at cool room temperature for about 15 minutes. Preheat the oven to 200°C/400°F/gas 6.

Heat a large non-stick frying pan over a high heat, add the partridge and cook until well seared all over. Transfer to a roasting tin and cook in the oven for 8–10 minutes. Remove from the oven and set aside.

Heat the remaining oil in a large, heavy-based frying pan, add the mustard seeds and cook until they crackle. Add the curry leaves, ginger, garlic and green chillies and cook, stirring frequently, until golden brown.

Add the remaining ginger and garlic paste and cook, stirring, for 2 minutes, then add the remaining chilli powder, the coriander and asafoetida and cook, stirring, for a further 2 minutes.

Stir in 2 tablespoons of the red chilli paste (any remaining chilli paste can be frozen and thawed when needed) and the vinegar and cook for 10–12 minutes until the oil separates. Add the partridge and check the seasoning. Leave to cool, then store in an airtight container in the fridge for 2 days before eating. The pickle will keep for up to a week in the fridge.

GAJRELLA

Carrots cooked in milk

SERVES 4

600 g/1 lb 5 oz carrots, grated

500 ml/18 fl oz full-fat milk

50 g/1¾ oz khoya (Indian milk cake) or condensed milk

150 g/5½ oz caster sugar

20 g/¾ oz melon seeds

½ teaspoon ground green cardamom

2 tablespoons ghee

20 g/¾ oz raw unsalted cashew nuts

20 g/¾ oz sultanas

vanilla ice cream, to serve

Put the grated carrots and milk in a heavy-based saucepan and bring to the boil, then cook over a medium heat until the milk evaporates, stirring frequently to prevent sticking.

Add half the khoya or condensed milk and cook until well blended. Add the sugar, melon seeds and cardamom and cook for 5–7 minutes. Stir in the remaining khoya or condensed milk and remove from the heat.

Heat the ghee in a separate saucepan, add the cashew nuts and sultanas and cook until golden brown. Strain through a sieve and drain on kitchen paper.

Add the cashews and sultanas to the carrot mixture and cook, stirring, for a further minute or so. Serve hot with vanilla ice cream.

JALEBI

Deep-fried batter coils in sugar syrup

SERVES 4

250 g/9 oz plain flour

30 g/1 oz semolina

1/4 teaspoon baking powder

85 g/3 oz thick natural yoghurt

1/2 teaspoon saffron threads, soaked in a little hot water for 20 minutes

500 g/1 lb 2 oz ghee

FOR THE SYRUP

500 g/1 lb 2 oz granulated sugar

1/2 teaspoon ground green cardamom

1 tablespoon kewra water

Put the flour, semolina, baking powder, yoghurt and saffron and its soaking water with 100 ml/3½ fl oz water in a large bowl and beat with a whisk until smooth. Cover with a clean damp tea towel and leave to ferment for 4–5 hours. Whisk the batter thoroughly again, then pour into a squeeze bottle.

To make the syrup, put the sugar, cardamom and kewra water with 700 ml/1¼ pints water in a wide heavy-based saucepan and bring to the boil. Cook for a about 3 minutes until a runny syrup forms.

Heat the ghee in a large frying pan to 180–190°C/350°–375°F, or until a cube of bread browns in 30 seconds. Squeeze in the batter in a steady stream to form a few separate coils and deep-fry until golden brown. Remove with a slotted spoon and transfer to a flat sieve, then immerse in the sugar syrup and leave for 1–1½ minutes to soak up. Remove and keep hot while you cook and soak the remainder of the batter.

LASSI

Chilled yoghurt drink with saffron and cardamom

SERVES 4

400 g/14 oz natural yoghurt

4 tablespoons caster sugar

½ teaspoon ground green cardamom

pinch saffron threads, soaked in a little hot water for 20 minutes

handful of ice cubes

Place the yoghurt, sugar, cardamom, saffron and its soaking water and ice cubes in a blender with 200 ml/7fl oz cold water. Blend until smooth and frothy, but be careful not to over-blend, as it will begin to thin down.

Pour into glasses and serve immediately.

GLOSSARY

Most of these ingredients are available online, in larger branches of mainstream supermarkets or specialist Indian grocers.

ajwain – also known as carom seeds, ajwain seeds are pale in colour and look like a smaller version of cumin seeds. They are highly fragrant and have a flavour of thyme.

amchoor – a citrus seasoning made from dried unripe mangoes. Also referred to as dried mango powder, it is used to flavour fruit salads, curries and dals. It can be used to tenderise meats, poultry and fish.

arbi – also known as eddo, taro, colocasia or Indian yam. Both the starchy, tuberous root (which looks similar to a potato) and the green leaves of the plant are edible. The root can be used in curries and stir-fries.

asafoetida – or asafetida. A gum produced from the sap of the roots of the ferula plant (a giant, odorous fennel). Although not native to India, it has been used in Indian cooking for centuries. It can be bought in pieces, powder form or granulated. It has a horrible smell when raw, but this smell dissipates once it has been cooked and adds an onion like flavour to the dish.

caraway – a Persian type of cumin that is used in the flavouring of bread, biscuits, cakes and cheeses.

carom seeds – see **ajwain**.

chana, roasted – roasted chana are black chickpeas that have been roasted, skinned and split. They have a wonderfully nutty flavour and are ground and added to chutneys and many other dishes.

charoli nuts – also known as chironji, the spice charoli tastes slightly of almonds. Primarily used in the creation of sweet dishes, they can also be used to thicken curry sauces and flavour batters.

chickpea flour – also known as gram flour or besan, is a flour made from ground chickpeas. It is the key ingredient in pakoras, bhajis and other dumplings and can also be used as a thickener.

edible silver or gold leaf – also known as vark or varq, this is made from pure gold or silver that has been hammered between leather pads until thinner than paper. The sheets are used on top of sweets and desserts and often as a garnish on top of dishes like biryani. The concept of eating gold and silver was invented by the 17th-century Mughal emperors.

fenugreek – a yellow spice (also called methi) that is the seed of the same name. It is used in the preparation of pickles, curry powders, pastes and breads. The leaf of the plant is also used, both as fresh leaves and as dried ones, which are usually added to a dish along with other whole spices.

garam masala – from the Hindi literally meaning 'hot mixture', it is a basic blend of common Indian spices which varies from region to region. Typically, it includes coriander seeds, cumin seeds, fennel seeds, black peppercorns, cloves, cardamom pods, mace, cinnamon or cassia bark and bay leaves.

ghee – clarified butter, made by boiling down a large amount of butter until all the water in it has evaporated and the impurities either sink to the bottom of the pan or float to the top. It is then strained and used in all sorts of dishes, often because it has a much higher smoking point than oil or butter.

gram flour – see **chickpea flour**.

gulkand – also known as gulqand, is a sweet preserve of rose petals made by layering sugar and petals in an airtight container and stirring occasionally. It is commonly used as an ingredient in paan, a popular dessert in India, Pakistan and Bangladesh.

hung yoghurt – natural live yoghurt, which has been strained through a cheese cloth or muslin cloth overnight in the fridge. Hang over a bowl to collect the liquid.

jaggery – also known as jaggeree. It is an unrefined whole cane sugar – a concentrated product of cane juice which has not had the molasses and crystals separated. Used in sweet dishes as well as savoury dals, jaggery can be replaced with soft brown sugar if not available.

kewra water – an extract from the pandanus flower which is used to flavour meats, drinks and desserts in India and Southeast Asia. Can be substituted with rose water if required.

khoya – also known as khoa. It is a milky substance similar in texture to ricotta cheese, but made from the whole milk rather than the whey. Khoya is used primarily is sweet dishes and can be used as a thickening agent.

kohlrabi – also known in India as noolkol, is a relative of the cabbage. It has large green leaves and a bulbous root – both of which are edible.

lauki – also known as bottle gourd, this is widely available in India. It has a pale green skin.

lotus puffs – also known as makhana or fox nut, these are the seeds of a plant from the lotus family, which has purple flowers not dissimilar to the lotus or waterlily flower. The plants are cultivated in ponds all over northern India; the kernels of the seed pod are then roasted or fried which causes them to puff like popcorn. They are often used in sweets and desserts, and can be eaten as a snack.

lotus stem – also known as lotus root, this is the edible rhizome of the lotus plant. It resembles a long cylindrical tuber but when sliced it reveals a delicate lacy crunch vegetable. It cannot be eaten raw and discolours once peeled, due to the high starch content.

panch phoran – a spice mix that includes five (panch) whole aromatic seeds. It can be used as a whole spice mix or used as a ground spice. The five spices are fennel seeds, black mustard seeds, cumin seeds, nigella seeds and fenugreek seeds.

paneer – a fresh cheese used throughout India. It is made by heating and curdling milk and then separating the solids (see page 202). It goes rubbery if left overnight so should always be made fresh. Alternatively it can be found in most good supermarkets.

papaya paste – a paste made from deseeded green papaya that has been blended with the skin still on.

parwal – also known as the pointed gourd or the green potato. This is used in soups, curries and sometimes sweet dishes. It is also popular when simply fried.

roasted chana – see **chana**.

tarka – also known as tadka, this is the process of infusing cooking oil by frying whole spices in a high heat to enhance the spice's flavours. This flavoured oil is then used as a dressing for dals, or can used as a base for cooking vegetables and meat. In some areas of India, specific spices are used and these include: cumin seeds, black mustard seeds, fennel seeds, fresh green chillies, dried red chillies, fenugreek seeds, asafoetida, cassia, cloves, curry leaves, chopped onion and garlic.

vadi/wadi – these are sun-dried lentil dumplings, used in both Punjabi cooking (wadi) and Bengali cooking (vadi).

INDEX

ACKNOWLEDGEMENTS

The authors would like to thank the following for making this book possible:

Karen Thomas – for using her wonderful creative vision and succeeding in the challenging task of bringing the recipe to life through her photographs. The final shots are more than we could have asked for!

Oliver Sinclair – for bringing the Grand Trunk Road to the UK and enjoying the project as much as we did. Your photographs capture the real India and allow everyone to feel the hustle and bustle and beauty of the place.

Jacqui Caulton – for truly understanding the concept of this book and creating a great design.

Clare Sayer – for allowing us to re-visit and share our experiences of India through this book. Thank you for believing in the project – it was only a matter of time this book would be created, and we thank you and New Holland for supporting us in making it happen.

Sunil Vijayakar – for capturing the essence of the dishes through your wonderful styling! A creative genius.

Liz Belton – for sourcing the props to perfectly complement the dishes.

James Bulmer and Frances Cottrell – for their expertise in the industry and for acting as a constant sounding board. Thank you for your enthusiasm and patience.

All the staff at Moti Mahal for their untiring support and dedication, especially when it came to testing the recipes. Particular thanks must go to Nirupama Palakonda.

We would also like to take the opportunity to thank the Choudhrie family for their unwavering support and commitment to the restaurant through thick and thin. You remind us what a pleasure it is to cook for people with an equal passion for food. I cannot thank you enough.

Finally, to every dhaba owner, street vendor, restaurant proprietor, chef, chai wallah and hawker along the Grand Trunk Road, past and present, for giving us the inspiration to create this book.

BC	01/12